A Tactical Ethic

A Tactical Ethic

moral conduct in the insurgent battlespace

Dick Couch

Author of *Chosen Soldier* and *The Sheriff of Ramadi*

NAVAL INSTITUTE PRESS
Annapolis, Maryland

Naval Institute Press
291 Wood Road
Annapolis, MD 21402

Library of Congress Cataloging-in-Publication Data

Couch, Dick, 1943–
A tactical ethic : moral conduct in the insurgent battlespace / Dick Couch.
   p. cm.
Includes bibliographical references and index.
ISBN 978-1-59114-137-2 (alk. paper)
1. War—Moral and ethical aspects. 2. Military ethics. I. Title.
U22.C68 2010
172'.42—dc22
                    2009047267

17 16 15 14 13 12 11 10   9 8 7 6 5 4 3 2
First printing

*This work is dedicated to all those American warriors
in the insurgent battlespace who,
at additional personal risk,
conduct themselves in a moral and righteous manner
in the service of their nation.*

Contents

Foreword

The best description of combat leadership I've read comes not from a military field manual or a serious work of history, but from a novel about the ancient Spartans. In *Gates of Fire*, author (and former U.S. marine) Steven Pressfield describes a Spartan officer in battle.

> I watched Dienekes, re-forming the ranks of his platoon, listing their losses and summoning aid for the wounded. . . . The Spartans have a term for that state of mind which must at all costs be shunned in battle. They call it katalepsis, possession, meaning that derangement of the senses that comes when terror or anger usurps dominion of the mind.

> This, I realized now watching Dienekes rally and tend to his men, was the role of the officer: to prevent those under his command, at all stages of battle—before, during, and after—from becoming "possessed." To fire their valor when it flagged and rein in their fury when it threatened to take them out of hand. That was Dienekes' job. That was why he wore the transverse-crested helmet of an officer.

> His was not, I could see now, the heroism of an Achilles. He was not a superman who waded invulnerably into the slaughter, single-handedly slaying the foe by myriads. He was just a man doing a job. A job whose primary attribute was self-restraint and self-composure, not for his own sake, but for those whom he led by his example.

Weapons and tactics change in warfare, but the human element in combat has remained largely the same across millennia: a good hoplite at Thermopylae in 480 BC would have looked a lot like a good cavalryman at Gettysburg in 1863 and a good infantryman in Helmand province in 2009. But popular portrayals of courage, aggressiveness, and loyalty are only half the story. Of equal importance are restraint, compassion, and honor—qualities no less central to strong combat leadership, though they may be less romantic, and less easily caricatured on television.

Dick Couch knows this better than most of us. A Naval Academy graduate and veteran of SEAL Team One in Vietnam (where he led one of the few successful POW rescue operations of that war), he writes with the hard-earned knowledge of personal experience. The essence of his message in *A Tactical Ethic* is that our warrior culture must embrace the same *passionate intolerance* for unlawful and immoral acts on the battlefield that it currently has for leaving a comrade behind, and that our junior leaders have a *continuous and never-ending duty* to make this so.

Captain Couch has served in operational combat units, and knows that these things are easy to say, but harder to do. When young Americans join our ground forces—the Army and Marine combat arms, and the special operations forces—they seek to join what General David Petraeus calls "the brotherhood of the close fight." They want to be part of the pack. Most have visions of glory and gunfights, not patience and proportionality. These aspects of military culture, however, are inextricably linked: true warriors must develop a firm moral platform from which they project power.

This obligation is borne most heavily by the commanders. The men who lead our teams, squads, platoons, and companies balance two often-conflicting demands: accomplishing their mission and taking care of their troops. In the heat of battle, when people are dying, it can be tempting to dismiss ethical considerations as a distant, and lesser, concern. That is wrong. Sound ethical conduct is absolutely essential to both mission accomplishment and troop welfare.

Doing the right thing is mission critical for at least three reasons. First, this is the era of the "strategic corporal." Because of globalized media and the presence of journalists on the battlefield, individual actions by junior warriors can have national, strategic repercussions—for good and for ill. Second, polls consistently show that the military is the most trusted institution in American life—more than the police, the church, and even the Supreme Court. Maintaining that trust is a sacred obligation that helps to ensure the public support our warriors need in order to win. Third, the successful conduct of counterinsurgency is often counterintuitive to the principles of conventional warfare. American counterinsurgency doctrine, for example, includes a series of seemingly paradoxical statements: the more force is used, the less effective it is; the more you protect your force, the less secure you may be; sometimes doing nothing is the best reaction. The theme uniting these principles is an overriding concern for the safety and welfare of the civilian population. They, rather than a piece of terrain or the enemy's forces, are the centers of gravity: protect them and persuade them, and we win; neglect them or kill them, and we lose.

Troop welfare—the duty to care for the sons and daughters entrusted to our combat leaders—likewise demands a strong tactical ethic. Every war eventually ends, and then the warriors revert to being private citizens again. They go on with their lives. Their leaders have a duty to do everything possible to ensure that they can look their children and grandchildren in the eye, and at themselves in the mirror, when talking about their service in wartime.

Given the centrality of tactical ethics to winning our fights and caring for our people, ethical training should not be separated from operational training. Moreover, training new recruits in the schoolhouse isn't enough. In order to succeed, ethical training must be a component of the tactical training that happens each day in small units throughout the military. Junior officers and NCOs—our nation's frontline combat leaders—are duty bound to build and maintain not only the technical competence of their units, but also their culture and their moral health. They do this not for their own sake, but, like Dienekes, for those whom they lead by their example.

Nathaniel C. Fick is the chief executive officer of the Center for a New American Security. He served as a Marine infantry officer in Afghanistan and Iraq and is the author of *One Bullet Away*.

Preface: The Issues

For most of 2004 and into 2005 I was living at Camp Mackall, North Carolina, the Army Special Forces training base near Fort Bragg. I was embedded with the students and training cadres for the Special Forces Qualification Course—better known as the SF Q-Course. The yearlong course had a lot of classroom work, but I spent many a night boring holes in the swamps of North Carolina with these Special Forces trainees. One day a young captain in the course sought me out. We were on a short break from training—training often conducted round the clock, seven days a week. This officer was an outgoing, personable officer, but I could see that he now had an uncertain and troubled expression on his face.

"Sir, do you have a minute?"

"Sure," I said, and we took a few steps away from the other trainees. Like many Army captains coming into Special Forces, he'd spent time in Iraq and Afghanistan.

"Sir, I've got something that's been bothering me, and I need to get it off my chest. I hope you don't mind my using you as a sounding board. And with your permission, I'd like it to go no further than between us."

"Very well," I replied. "Fire away."

"My last tour was in northern Afghanistan, where I served as the Army liaison officer to some of our special missions units. We were at an isolated base—really not much more than an airstrip and some crude huts." He did not say which unit, but I could only guess that he was referring to a SEAL special missions unit. My background was well known to him. "One evening this unit brought back an Afghan fighter they'd taken out of a village that was known to support the

Taliban. After a brief interrogation by the intel guys, they gave this Afghan back to the unit that had captured him—apparently he was of little value. He was just another local male with an AK-47 and a surly attitude. Well, sir, they took him out back, away from the camp, and they beat him to death." He went into some detail as to what took place, but that was basically the gist of it. Apparently only two of the Americans did the beating, but the others in the unit did nothing to stop it.

After a moment I asked, "What did you do?" I wondered if he had reported it.

"Not much I could do," he said. "I tried to stop it, but was told to clear off—that it was none of my business. I think they would have shot me had I pressed the issue. As for reporting it, it would have been their word against mine, and there were eight or ten of them." He told me when it happened and where it happened, but did not say who.

"What would you like me to do?" I asked.

He thought for a moment. "I don't really know, sir. Things like this shouldn't happen. It may not be right on my part, but I don't want to get involved. I just want to finish my training here, get to my Special Forces group, and get back to the fight." He paused again. "I guess I just needed to tell someone."

I thought about this information for several days. This was a very fine officer; he was bright, capable, and patriotic. I believed him. Not knowing what else to do, I sought out a senior special operations officer I knew well; I have some close senior contacts in the U.S. Special Operations Command. I repeated the story to him.

"Do you have any more specifics, like who was involved, by name?" he asked me. I said I didn't, and that the individual who witnessed this was very reluctant to come forward. "Well, then, there's not much we can do. To move on this, I'd have to have specific information and a sworn statement. There is nothing I can do."

Nor was there anything I could do but to remind my friend that we were lucky this Army captain elected to bare his soul to me, rather than some reporter from the *New York Times*. So there it rested—and has rested since I learned of it. Prior to this disturbing story, I had heard of other incidents, and I've heard about many more since. Most, but not all, were of lesser consequence. This story had been about murder, not a wrong shooting in the fog of war. And it got me thinking. How much of this takes place in the active theaters? How much of it goes unreported? Since the conflicts in Iraq and Afghanistan have metastasized into insurgencies, our role has devolved into one of security, counterinsurgency, and training. This can be frustrating, and frustration can lead to wrong conduct. This kind of wrong conduct is very costly—in terms of those wronged, in the erosion of our warrior ethos, and in the damage to our mission objectives in the insurgent battlespace. And what can be done to correct this wrong and dysfunctional behavior? I believe our senior military commanders are aware that wrong conduct has taken place and continues to take place in the active theaters. I also believe they take it very seriously and are working to prevent it. The military culture is a hierarchical one, and these commanders almost have to take a top-down approach. However, I believe this is an issue of small-unit tactical ethics on the battlefield, or lack thereof, and its solution is best addressed from the bottom up.

Tactical ethics, by my own definition, is the moral and ethical armor that accompanies our warriors into battle. It applies to the engaged unit as well as to the individual. The Laws of Land Warfare and theater-specific rules of engagement (ROEs) define the legal combat boundaries within which our warriors must function. Tactical ethics augment these legal constraints. Together, they define the limits and structure—the permissions and the prohibitions—that govern the lethal work of combat. They allow the warrior to take life in the name of his nation and his profession, and they guide him in issues of discrimination and proportionality in the use of force. This is true for all in the military who take up professional arms in the service of their nation, but in this work I will focus on ground-combat warriors, specifically the soldiers, marines, and special operators who engage in ground combat. In the current insurgent conflicts and those that may be in our future, they are the ones who carry the fight to our enemies.

This ethical armor that I will be addressing is both offensive and defensive. It is offensive in that ground combat involves pursuing the enemy and taking life. Even if cloaked with the moral authority of national service, the taking of human life is serious business. It is to be done judiciously and within proscribed limits. Those who oppose us must know that we will professionally and expeditiously bring about their rightful destruction. As a nation we are very accomplished at this. Our military has the talent and the technology to take life just about anywhere, anytime. Our warriors are very good. So good, in fact, that in many cases it is only our legal and self-imposed moral restraint that determines whether an enemy fighter lives or dies.

This ethical armor is also defensive in that it protects the goodness and humanity of our warriors; they go into battle for us, and we, the beneficiaries of their service, must do all in our power to see them repatriated humanely and with honor. So we as a nation must ensure that our military projects its force in a right and just manner—that the behavior of our warriors on the battlefield is in keeping with certain moral boundaries. This is for our sake and for the sake of our warriors. And, for the record, legal coverage for a lethal act is not moral coverage. The legal and the moral may often overlap, but no matter what the lawyers may say, they are not the same. To quote the noted Canadian historian Dr. Michael Ingatieff, "moral decisions are simply too important to be left up to lawyers."

The issues of right conduct on the battlefield are complex and, by nature, highly discriminatory. There are rules, but these rules must be applied in a dynamic and dangerous environment. Following these rules relates to proper preparation—the right professional *and* moral training. It also relates to good leadership. With an occasional exception, today's battlefield is an insurgent battlefield. Most of what gets done on this modern battlefield is done at the squad and platoon level—in combat units of two to forty. Battlefield decisions are made by junior officers and mid- to senior-grade noncommissioned officers—that is, senior enlisted men. They govern battlefield conduct, and, to a great extent, they decide who lives and dies. And this is why tactical ethics is a bottom-up business.

There are three considerations that are never far from the mind of a commander in an active theater who has squads and platoons in the field:

The value of the target—collectively, the mission
The risk to his own troops
The risk to noncombatant civilians

A lot of time and attention, and no small amount of lost sleep, go into balancing these issues, both the tactical considerations as well as moral considerations. They have a close relationship in conventional battle and maneuver warfare, but they are especially interconnected in insurgent wars—the ones we are now fighting. Regarding insurgent war, this is how our enemies will engage *us*. Since our enemies have neither our talent nor our technology, nor our moral framework, insurgency is their combat of choice. Many say our insurgent enemies have no moral grounding. My view is that they have a different moral reference and urgency to *their* cause—considerations that make their actions immoral from *our* perspective, a related issue but not our focus here. This is not a text on jihad or counterinsurgency warfare, but I will say without qualification that the prize on the insurgent battlefield is the human terrain. We win the people, we win the battle; we lose the people, and it's a defeat. How we treat noncombatants is very important. Since the enemy is often close to the people, their numbers drawn from local populations, or is hiding within that population, how we treat captured enemy combatants also becomes important. Our conduct and how we treat civilians during the fighting and in the important postcombat phases of an insurgency are critical to mission success. For this reason, close attention to the third consideration listed above takes on added meaning.

Every action on the insurgent battlefield has consequence. On the kinetic side, shooting an armed Egyptian with ties to al-Qaeda just outside Baghdad is pretty straightforward. Killing a young local militiaman on the street a few blocks from his home is something else. There may have been a legal and moral justification for the bullet each received, but the consequence of shooting a local youth may be far more dramatic. Was he a hard-core insurgent or just a kid on the street brandishing an AK-47 to prove himself? Was he a willing or unwilling participant? How will his extended family receive the news of his death? Will his father, brothers, and uncles now join the insurgency as a result of our shooting the young man? On the nonkinetic side, every time a convoy or string of armored Humvees rumbles through a village, the residents must move aside, and all local vehicles have to leave the road and assume a nonthreatening attitude. Every time a soldier or a marine engages Iraqis or Afghans on the street, or enters their neighborhoods or homes, there is a chance for disrespect and effrontery. All this places a heavy responsibility on our young warriors and our junior battlefield leaders. Right action on the insurgent battlefield can be very nuanced. To carry out their mission they must operate in a lethal environment with restraint. It's not always easy.

Quite simply, the care and restraint with which we use military force on the insurgent battlefield, and especially how we treat noncombatants, is a vital part of the mission. This same care and restraint can also put our troops more at risk. Our success or failure in Iraq, and future Iraqs, will be a balancing act between lethality and restraint; it's the nature of counterinsurgent warfare. If we are to win these battles, we have to win the people. That means we must insist on right conduct on the part of our soldiers, marines, and special operators, and that we must ask these same warriors to assume that additional risk as they tend to the well-being of noncombatants. Again, this can be very challenging and difficult.

Before going further, it might be helpful if I identify what I mean by right conduct and wrong conduct on this battlefield. First, the right conduct. This involves taking life within the narrowly defined

Laws of Land Warfare and theater-imposed rules of engagement—
the ROEs. If the guy is shooting at you, he has forfeited his right to
life and has earned himself a bullet. Past that, there will be restrictions, and these restrictions will be situational. When can we take
life—when should we take a life? If the enemy is armed and moving
with tactical intent—probably. Simply moving with tactical intent,
armed with only a cell phone—possibly. Just armed—possibly.
Killing them all and letting God sort them out—not an option on
the insurgent battlefield. Since the prize of this fight is the people,
every death has consequence. In the context of our warriors, every
death has strategic and moral significance. Yet it's not always simply
a matter of discrimination in the context of combatants—who gets
a bullet and who does not.

Our treatment of noncombatants is critical to mission success. There will inevitably be collateral damage—loss of property and civilians inadvertently killed as a result of the conflict.
On our side, this is sometimes unavoidable and/or unintended.
On the part of our enemies, it may be an element of their strategy. Yet even when insurgents use terror and knowingly kill
civilians, it can be laid at our doorstep. We are in *their* country,
and our presence can be linked to the violence and their lack
of security. This is the nature of insurgent warfare "over there."
While there are inherent disadvantages to being an expeditionary force in an insurgency, there are things we *can* do—right
conduct that promotes our interests and our agenda. We can help
provide for local security, and that often involves duties similar
to those of policemen. We can respect the local culture and the
norms of that society. When we enter the locals' neighborhoods
and homes, we can do so with proper respect and deference.
A foreign armed presence is implicitly offensive. We must do
all in our power to balance the negative impact of our presence
with our own need for force protection. Counterinsurgency doctrine requires that we maintain security only until we can train
local security forces to do the job. When the local police are on
the streets and we are not, we win.

Wrong conduct on the battlefield involves everything from offending the locals due to our lack of cultural understanding to harassment and to indiscriminate killing. It could be something as simple as entering an Arab household with your left foot instead of your right, or not taking the time to learn the appropriate greeting in the local language. But wrong conduct also includes indiscriminate shooting, killing livestock, and damaging property. It includes firing near civilians and tossing concussion grenades in their proximity without provocation. It includes training weapons on them or forcing them to take submissive measures unnecessarily. Admittedly there is often a fine line between force protection (personal and collective self-defense) and arrogant behavior. When it's the latter, it threatens the mission and unravels hard-won trust we may have struggled for years to establish with the locals. Is this wrong and wanton behavior widespread? I don't believe it is. Yet, in speaking with a great number of warriors returning from the battlespace, I'm convinced it goes on far more than is reported. This kind of behavior, while unrepresentative of command intent and the conduct of the majority, is still unacceptable. I won't go so far as to say it is commonplace, but it does happen, and I believe that it is far too often condoned. This wrong conduct demeans those warriors who, at some personal risk, do conduct themselves properly. Furthermore, it is the worst possible insult to those fellow warriors who have fallen in this battle.

All this may seem a startling indictment of our force projection capability and the conduct of our troops. Perhaps so. As stated above, I believe that this wrong behavior is not the intent of our deployed senior commanders or the American military establishment. It is not the norm of those who serve in our armed forces. But it is, in my opinion, an ongoing and troubling issue. It threatens our ability to engage insurgent enemies, and it threatens our image in the world. Sadly, I believe the origins of this issue are in the social fabric of our nation, the darker aspects of our military culture, and the evolving issues of trust, honor, and loyalty within our warrior culture. It is the duty of our nation and our senior military commanders to put this right. It is the duty of our junior officers and senior noncommissioned officers to put this right. I would go so far as to say it is job one. We simply must find a way to uniformly improve the moral and ethical conduct of our warriors. *A Tactical Ethic* will examine these issues and offer some ideas and methodologies to address them.

Author's special note: As we explore this important and sensitive subject, I need to make one thing very clear. It may at times seem like I'm speaking from my ethical high horse—some kind of a born-again, moral academic who has lost touch with the contemporary battlefield. Some may contend that it's a new world, a new threat, and a new conflict. This may be the case, but I believe the mistakes we are making in Iraq and Afghanistan are the same mistakes we made forty years ago in Vietnam. This I know from firsthand experience. I was there, and I made some of those mistakes. But Vietnam was a sideshow in the Cold War; we lost that battle, but we won the war. If Iraq and Afghanistan slip away, these battles will put us on the brink of losing a war we dare not to lose.

Acknowledgments

I'd like to thank my former colleagues in the Leadership, Ethics, and Law Department at the U.S. Naval Academy, who continue to strive to make Honor, Courage, Commitment more than just words for our future Navy and Marine Corps leaders. I'd also like to thank the midshipmen I was privileged to have had in my classes at the Academy; the teacher always learns more than the students. And, finally, I'd like to thank Jim Gullickson, my trusted copy editor, who guided me through yet another book, and Susan Corrado of the Naval Institute Press, who put it all together.

CHAPTER ONE

A Careful Approach to the Issues

During the midsummer of 2008 I accepted a position to return to the U.S. Naval Academy, this time as an instructor. I arrived in Annapolis in August to take up my new duties. It was good to be back at the "boat school," as we graduates often refer to the Academy. Many things had changed since my midshipmen days some forty years ago, but like any tradition-bound institution, there was also much as I remembered it.

This was not my first time back. For a number of years, I have returned to the Naval Academy to lecture on special operations, counterinsurgency, and creative writing. However, this was my first true classroom duty as a full-time professor. Teaching Naval Academy midshipmen is a wonderful experience. They are bright, respectful, attentive, and, for the most part, eager to learn. In anticipation of this classroom duty, I recalled a 2003 interview with Victor Davis Hanson, who at the time was a tenured professor at California State University, Fresno. He too came to Annapolis on a sabbatical of sorts to teach for a year. He made an interesting comparison between Fresno State students and midshipmen at the Naval Academy. At Fresno State (an institution for which he holds a high regard) Hanson described lecture classes of two hundred or more students. They dressed as they pleased and often brought food and drinks with them to the lecture hall. Many were tardy and not a few left early, and if they had been studying late or out partying the night before, they just might take a few moments during the lecture to rest their eyes. They could attend class, or not, as they wished. He described Fresno State as a good school that produced graduates who go on to do important and useful work, but he didn't refer to what he did there as education. At the Naval Academy his experience, as my own, was not like that. Our class sections are fourteen to seventeen midshipmen, who are very seldom late to class and never absent without official permission, usually granted in advance. When class begins, the section leader calls the students to attention and reports the class formed, noting any absentees. Sleeping is not allowed. When the bell rings at the end of the session, no one moves until the instructor releases the class. The section leader again calls the students to their feet and dismisses them. The midshipmen come to class ready to learn in a system tailored for instruction. If the learning does not take place, then it's all on me, the instructor.

My course was Moral Reasoning for Military Leaders. It's more commonly referred to as the Ethics Course. I've always had an interest in ethics as it relates to battlefield conduct, specifically the battlefield conduct of our deployed special operations warriors—Navy SEALs, Army Special Forces, and the like. In all of my nonfiction works, I've written about what I often call the battlefield ethos, and in some of my books I've addressed it in some detail. To be candid, I've been a little Pollyannaish about it, speaking to this ethos in a positive way and citing best practices in both training and operational contexts. This was not difficult, nor was it untruthful. Within our special operations forces (SOF) components, and indeed all of our armed forces, there are some magnificent warriors whose professionalism and attention to duty are exceptional. Their moral calibration and conduct, on and off the battlefield, is in keeping with all that we expect of our best fighters. But there have been lapses, notable ones. What happened with the Army at Abu Ghraib, the Marines at Haditha, and our SOF components in Afghanistan seriously damaged our international image; the lingering ghosts of those incidents continue to threaten our mission in the active theaters. And while these incidents may seem to be as isolated as they are costly, I believe inappropriate acts have taken place—and are taking place—more often than those that have become breaking news stories. I've spoken with a number of our soldiers, marines, and special operators, and while they're most reluctant to talk out of school, there seem to be undercurrents in our military, isolated subcultures, if you will, that allow for immoral and unlawful conduct. Bottom line, I believe it happens more often than we know it does, and more than we would like to think it does.

Whenever I speak of wrong action on the battlefield, and in some cases extremely bad conduct, I'm frequently asked to cite specific examples—who, where, and when. In this work I will *not* go into specific detail or identify wrongdoers or the reporters of wrongdoing. While I have neither a cleric's collar nor a physician's shingle, I am a writer and have a responsibility to those who have taken me into their confidence. This is a painful issue. I know there are good commanders in our military who wish not to speak publicly about this subject and are as concerned as I am. I think General David Petraeus is more than aware of the problem. While he must be circumspect in his remarks, and certainly so in deference to the many thousands of good soldiers under his command, I believe his letter to the troops dated 10 May 2007 (see Appendix I) speaks directly to the issue of wrong conduct on the battlefield. It also addresses the difficulties in sorting out the wrong actions from the righteous ones within the "brotherhood of the close fight."

The wrong, and even criminal, conduct of American servicemen is never an easy topic to bring up, as it tends to color the many with the bad actions of a few. In light of that, some would say why write a book on the subject, that these incidents are a collateral damage of war or that these are problems that should be addressed in-house. There are those who might even argue that the incidents of reported criminal conduct are untrue, or that they are so isolated as to be nonrepresentative of our deployed personnel. Even if this were to be the case, the potential harm of even isolated wrong conduct on the battlefield is immense. I'm of the belief that wrong things have taken place, are taking place, and are *not* being adequately addressed. These illegal and immoral actions should never happen; we can do better. We owe it to the overwhelming number of our soldiers who do the right thing all the time, every time. Still, it's not without some sense of reservation that I've chosen to write this book. I believe there are conditions in place, typically at the small-unit level (company-, platoon-, and squad-size units), that allow for the emergence of some very dysfunctional and harmful conduct. The potential damage simply cannot be ignored. It's a mission-critical issue as well as a moral issue.

Our military, as a component of our society and as a profession, is held in great regard by our nation. Surveys show that the military is held in higher esteem than the police, the medical profession, educators, judges, and many other professionals, including the civilian political authorities to which our military reports. As I said, the conduct of the vast majority of our soldiers, marines, and special operators is right and proper. For the most part they make good and humane choices on the battlefield—even assuming additional risk in making those choices and in executing their responsibilities. I need also to point out that command policy, tactical directives, and rules of engagement forbid the kind of conduct I'm addressing. Those who commit these acts are clearly operating outside of the legal and moral constraints of standing military orders and the norms of our warrior culture.

So what kind of specific conduct am I talking about? Is it an indiscretion or an atrocity—a result of the fog of war or criminal activity? A judgment call in the heat of battle is one thing; willful, wanton, and ongoing bad behavior is something else. And what are the conditions that allow for this kind of thing to take place? As I've already outlined, bad conduct ranges from indiscriminate shooting to the mistreatment of noncombatants. The conditions in which wrongful acts can occur typically arise when a few morally bankrupt individuals in a unit manage, or are allowed, to gain traction with other members of the unit. Quite often these bad apples are tactically proficient and even courageous, which makes their influence that much greater, their personal currency with other members of the unit more compelling. I've heard this condition described as the pirate factor, and in this text I'll often refer to those who wield such influence as pirates. These pirates, like those who infest the waters off the Horn of Africa, near the Somali coast, thrive when there is no effective counterbalance. They are corrosive moles who can poison the small-unit warrior culture. Too frequently a few pirates manage to gain a measure of influence or control in a small unit. And one might ask whether in a squad of ten soldiers, if two of are bad actors, does this mean the other eight are corrupt as well? Not really. But loyalty in a small unit is a powerful force. The pirates may co-opt a few men or none at all, but their influence is such, or perhaps their proficiency on the battlefield is such, that their wrong conduct is tolerated. So we must consider the system as well as the individuals. It may not be just a few bad apples in the barrel; it may be that we have a barrel that allows for both good and bad apples.

This undercurrent of immoral and illegal behavior, isolated as it might be, is very hard to root out and correct. Small-unit cultures are very tight-bonded. Basically no one wants to rat out his fellow teammate, and from his perspective, for good reason. He often feels the cure is worse than the crime. The media, rightfully or wrongfully, is not looking for incidences of right conduct or judicious applications of force. They want scandal. The troops know this, and so does the leadership up the chain of command. Even a good junior leader, when he is made aware of a wrongful shooting, will think twice before reporting it to his superiors. Why trash the good men under you, and the entire unit, for the actions of a few pirates? And to discipline them severely, as they should be, will require a formal set of charges. This is war; things get broken and people get killed. *Do I,* the lieutenant may ask himself, *want the aggravation and inconvenience of an investigation? Do I want my good soldiers to be tarred with this brush? Do the captain and colonel want this?* So the good lieutenant may elect *not* to peruse formal proceedings. He may opt for some nonjudicial punishment or verbal admonition. And the pirates will have gotten away with it—again. Sadly, they know they can get away with it, and so does everyone else in the unit. I don't wish to be too harsh on the lieutenant or the senior sergeant; it takes courage to run one of your troops up the flagpole. This is especially true when it generates pain for yourself, your chain of command, and everyone around you. I believe it's safe to say that illegal and immoral acts that may be taking place in the battlespace are being done under the radar of the senior leadership. It may be that on occasion a junior or field-grade officer or a senior enlisted leader has gone to the "dark side," or has been so incompetent as to be unaware of what's happening around him. But formal censure of bad activity is usually held in check by the threat of collateral damage to good soldiers.

Other questions that might be asked have to do with how such undesirable conduct is viewed when taken into historical context. Is this something new? Has this gone on in past wars? If so, to what degree? I have no way to measure this on a relative scale, but if I had to guess, I would say less so now than in the past. My only real frame of reference is our last protracted engagement—Vietnam. There, we know it happened. The massacre at My Lai in 1968 was a moral and military tragedy of immense proportions—perhaps the apex of wrong conduct in modern insurgency warfare. Even by Abu Ghraib standards it was a military and national scandal—close to 250 unarmed noncombatants slaughtered by armed American warriors. While it may be unrepresentative of warriors of that era—*my* era—it required the participation of an *entire company*. And there was a command structure in place that may not have condoned the action, but certainly tried to cover it up. Warrant Officer Hugh Thompson, who tried to intervene and reported the incident, was shunned by his brother warriors for years after. I think many of us just wanted to put the My Lai incident in the rearview mirror as quickly as possible. Perhaps that's why it was not until *1998* that our nation recognized the gallantry of Hugh Thompson with a much-deserved Distinguished Flying Cross.

It makes one wonder—what went on in Vietnam that went unreported and that we never knew about?

If Vietnam was the first war in which TV cameras roamed the battlespace, then Iraq and Afghanistan are the first extended struggles in which digital imaging, text messaging, and cell-phone cameras are commonplace. Today there is far more opportunity for a bad act to be reported—in some form or at least on some level. I've personally seen some rather disturbing e-mails from the deployed warriors. None of this happened forty years ago. when there were only a few reporters in theater and only a few soldiers carried Kodak Instamatic cameras. Mass access to cyberspace brings about greater, if informal, transparency. As for the world wars and Korea, we know wrong conduct took place, in squads and platoons and at the highest levels (if we want to count unrestricted aerial warfare). We won the two world wars, so we convened the war-crimes tribunals, and as winners may have avoided scrutiny of our own conduct. In Korea we fought to a draw in a short, vicious conflict that we seemed to prefer to get past as quickly as possible, emotionally and politically. Perhaps most important, these pre-Vietnam wars were engagements of main-force armies in which ground and infrastructure, not the people, were the military objectives. These may prove to have been the last of our major noninsurgent conflicts.

So why then, if the incidents of bad behavior may occur less often today than in past wars, should we be concerned? If it's simply a matter of the overreporting of an isolated, perhaps dwindling number of incidents, isn't this just a public relations problem? Maybe we should police the Internet a little better (the Chinese approach), or issue fewer press credentials in the battlespace. Even so, per my earlier comments, I do feel strongly that this is an issue that needs immediate attention and corrective action. Our future expeditionary posture may not be what it is now, but I don't see us ever without some form of military engagement overseas. There are any number of reasons for us to attend to the ethical health of our warrior culture, reasons which we will be exploring in this text. But chief among them is that they threaten the mission. As in Vietnam, we are in a struggle for the people. Again, it's insurgency warfare. The day we occupied Kabul and Baghdad, we began the battle for the human terrain. This is not a book about how slow we were to realize this or how badly we got it wrong; there is no shortage of books on these subjects. Nor is there profit in this discussion to ask why it took so long for us to get it right, if indeed we are getting it right. It's about how we can and must do better.

Because an insurgency is a war for the people, our conduct and our ideas matter. The use of excess force, violations of human rights, and abuse of civilians, even if they go unreported, cost us dearly in terms of achieving our goals and accomplishing our mission. Bad acts in maneuver warfare don't register on the scorecard nearly so much as they do in an insurgency.

So what can we do to change this? How can we bring the incident level of illegal and unethical acts to zero? I believe this has to do with close attention to our small-unit leadership and small-unit culture. Both have to be considered in the light of better training for junior leaders and better professional training of our tactical units—training that marries tactical skill sets with ethical skill sets. That said, leadership can only do so much; perhaps, more than anything else, this is a cultural issue. Within our warrior culture, we cherish and value the notion that we will leave no one behind on the battlefield—that if one of our own goes missing or is taken prisoner, we will go to great risk to bring him, or his remains, home. The kind of *passionate intolerance* for abandoning a brother warrior to the enemy must be applied to unlawful and immoral acts on the battlefield. In a sense, we *are* abandoning our fallen warriors if we ignore the immoral conduct of some of our warriors in the current battlespace. As for our repatriated warriors, they will at some time, or some future date, have to personally reconcile their past deeds to themselves. It may surface as post-traumatic stress, dysfunction in their role of spouse or father, or a life poorly lived. So, in some respects, the mission (the war) as well as the warrior is at risk.

While the "cure," if you will, must be applied at the basic tactical level, the formulation and application of this cure has to be a high priority for our senior military leaders. Iraq and Afghanistan are close-run issues. As of this writing, both could go either way. I'm concerned that the outcome of both may be influenced by wrong battlefield conduct. I'm also concerned that the negative baggage of tolerated, condoned wrong conduct may follow us from these conflicts to the next one. We simply must do that which is necessary to purge ourselves of the wrongdoers—the pirates. And we must find a way to avoid future piratelike behavior.

Looking at it another way, those whom I've labeled as pirates are, in their own way, insurgents. They seek to influence, if not control, the warrior culture; they want acceptance, or at least tolerance, of their bad behavior. All too often, they get it. So it's their misbehavior *and* their brother warriors' moral neutrality that is at the heart of the issue. To put it more accurately, those who willfully engage in unlawful and immoral conduct on the battlefield are giving aid and comfort to the enemy. They are traitors. Those who tolerate this conduct on the part of their brother warriors are, by their inaction, aiding and abetting that conduct. If awareness as to the consequence of inappropriate behavior becomes a part of our warrior culture, then issues of misplaced loyalty can be dealt with more effectively.

Once again, this is tough business. Americans like to think of their serving military as noble and worthy; we might hate war, but we love our warriors. So the notion that their conduct is not all it should be runs counter to our perception of those in uniform. I can assure you that, having taken on this project, it's much easier to speak about their virtues and write about their courage on the battlefield than to challenge it. I'm privileged to know, respect, and admire many of these warriors, primarily in the special operations community. They have no peer on this or any past field of battle. The Navy SEALs of my generation stand well in the shadow of the current generation of SEALs, and the shadow they cast is indeed a large one—an impressive one. My sense is that this modern professional upgrade is true for other special operations units and other active ground-force components. So as I bend to the task in seeking a more elevated moral platform for our warriors, it is to guard and serve the honorable majority that I take strong issue with the actions of a few. Where possible, my focus will be on what can be done in the future rather than what took place in the past. Yet having said that, an honest and sober inventory of existing culture and causation is key to understanding what is broken and what we might do to fix it. This system of warrior training and force projection isn't broken per se, but it can be made a great deal better with careful analysis and refinement.

A Tactical Ethic will explore the ethical "equipment" our soldiers currently take into battle, the deficiencies, as I see them, in their existing moral body armor, and what changes for the better might be put into place. As the title would imply, this work seeks to address a tactical moral imperative for the man in the arena—the marine on patrol, the soldier training indigenous forces, and the special operator preparing to engage a high-value target. The goal here is to investigate, and perhaps promote, a heightened state of moral awareness in order to (1) complement the advanced technical and ground-combat capabilities our warriors now enjoy and (2) complement the skills needed to succeed in the insurgent, human-terrain battlespace. Simply put, the moral and spiritual conditioning of our warriors has not kept pace with the technological advances and operational capabilities of our armed forces. Their moral lapses, as I mentioned earlier, have cost us dearly in terms of mission success and public opinion. To help the modern warrior in resisting the impulse to commit wrongful or immoral acts, we need to rethink how such warriors are made in the first place. In this work, I will refer to the "Inner Warrior." The concept behind this term fits nicely into what I think needs to be accomplished. The Inner Warrior is, I believe, a product of the conditioning of that moral fabric within all of us that makes the American warrior both effective and splendid.

The term "Inner Warrior" is not mine. I'm borrowing it from the Close Quarters Defense Academy, and then only with the permission of its founder, Duane Dieter. Much of the military "values/ethos training" I have observed has been separate and distinct from operational tactical training. It seems that we devote classroom time to ethics and case study, then gear up and go into the field on maneuvers at other times. Learning marksmanship, fire-and-movement, and close-quarters battle are currently unconnected to the notion of core beliefs and spiritual development that should be a key element in modern warrior training. It is my belief that professional skill-set training and moral conditioning should be complementary and integrative, both in the schoolhouse, in garrison, and on the battlefield. Here, I'm not advocating that we break up into discussion groups in the kill house, nor are we looking for warrior monks or even some parity of the philosophical and the martial. But professional skill and ethical conduct must be made to be symbiotic in training and application. I contend that a warrior's performance on the battlefield is not only complemented, but also enhanced, by a firm moral foundation. Ethics and martial skills can and should be part of the same training package and the same deployment package.

I've mentioned the Close Quarters Defense Academy. The disciplines developed and taught there may prove an excellent lens through which to consider a more rigorous approach to the ethical and moral grounding of our warriors. The CQD systems as developed by Duane Dieter are the best integration of the ethical and the tactical I have found to date. Currently moral and ethical training of our service ground-combat components is front-loaded. Values and warrior ethos training is most apparent in the boot camps—Marine entry-level training, Army basic/infantry training, and special operations qualification training. This kind of training tails off after the entry-level schools. Close Quarters Defense handles this differently. The CQD systems stress moral values while teaching advanced, close-quarters battle tactics; it's a marriage of professional skills and moral conditioning that addresses the war our soldiers, marines, and special operators sometimes face on a daily basis, which is a fight to the death.

Their world is an ambiguous and unforgiving environment. The needs of insurgency warfare require that our warriors move instantly from deadly force to restraint, then compassion, and back to deadly force. It's not easy, but it is mission critical.

An analysis of these battlefield requirements and recommended methods for improving them will be handled in the following chapters of this work. First, we will review the historical and social aspects of the rules we now ascribe to modern warfare. This will be a historical sprint, beginning with Saint Thomas Aquinas (1225–1274), who first held that we fight most righteously and justly (and morally) in defense of our families, neighbors, and communities. Most modern war theory and just-war theory begins with Thomas' rational for the taking of life. The two world wars brought us case law through war-crimes tribunals (winners trying the losers) and agreed-upon boundaries for conduct in war with the Geneva Conventions in 1949. Most of the precedent under which we currently conduct war was established in the twentieth century. All of this leads us to the rules, accepted practice, boundaries, and expected conduct of our troops on the modern battlefield—more specifically the insurgent battlefield. Currently we are engaged with an enemy who does not hold with our accepted practice of war. There are unique challenges in "playing by the rules" while engaging an enemy who does not.

Ethics and moral practice are taught in each of our service academies and at our military war colleges. Our basic and advanced training venues all include moral training. Our in-theater forces are briefed extensively on their rules of engagement. General David Petraeus' manual on counterinsurgency (FM 3-24 of December 2006, chapter 7) addresses battlefield conduct in some detail (see Appendix IV). Just-war theory and the Laws of Land Warfare make for good classroom discussion, and the general's manual provides excellent command guidance, but they are not enough. Several important questions still remain: How does this play out on today's battlefield with today's soldiers—in the deployed squads and platoons? How does values/ethos training translate into right conduct on the insurgent battlefield? Is it as effective as it could be or should be? How does all this guide the conduct of our warriors in Iraq, Afghanistan, and the next insurgency?

Since the low ebb of Abu Ghraib, a great deal of attention in the form of directives, inspections, briefings, and operational scrutiny has been put in place. Certainly at the highest levels there is more awareness of the negative consequences of such conduct. I do believe that Abu Ghraib was more of an isolated incident than a tip-of-the-iceberg thing. It was a top-down leadership issue that has been well documented. My concerns with Abu Ghraib involve the number of individuals on the lower end of the chain of command who were willing to follow illegal orders, and the number who simply looked the other way while the abuses were taking place. There will always be wrongdoers, in our society and our military. What worries me is the number of those who willing to tolerate wrongdoing in their presence. It's this kind of tolerance at the squad and platoon level that concerns me. Out in the field, tolerance for inappropriate action directly affects the civilian populations we must bring over to our side if we are to win our current wars. It's something we will deal with in this text in some detail.

One of the key components of ethical conduct in general, and certainly on the battlefield, is the answer to a simple question: what do you do when no one is looking? I've spoken with a number of soldiers, marines, and special operators, and for the most part they adhere to the conventions and restrictions. But not always—and, in some isolated cases, they seldom comply with the rules of engagement and the rules of common decency. Quite often what they're asked to do—and, in fairness to many of these brave soldiers, what they would like to do—puts them at risk. In some cases right conduct and restraint put our soldiers at more risk than they would like to assume. Seldom do they link this greater assumption of risk to mission success. And I acknowledge the difference in bending a rule in favor of better force protection and outright harassment of the locals. Both happen. The former is unfortunate but understandable; the latter is unacceptable.

Any discussion of the character of our warriors leads us to a discussion of the American character. We can send our soldiers on deployment out of America, but we can't take America out of our soldiers—not entirely. What is the individual and collective moral compass of our young men when they enter the military? How is that moral compass influenced by existing training programs? Once in the battlespace, how do the rigors of insurgency warfare, the conduct of the enemy, service cultures, peer pressure, and command climate influence their conduct on the battlefield? And, finally, are our soldiers, marines, and special operators conducting themselves as we, the nation, feel they should, or have they adopted a more expedient or peer-driven code of conduct? In short, how is all this playing out in the alleys of Sadr City and the foothills of the Hindu Kush?

Generation Kill. The title of the book and recent TV series offers some insights into the ground we need to cover. As for the book, it is a window into the culture and virtue of our young warriors. I find their trash talk and some of their attitudes alarming. I also find their courage and proficiency astounding. Secretary Donald Rumsfeld was fond of the saying "You go to war with the military you have." I would take that a step further: *you go to war with the generation you can put in the field*. We are in a war and have no other choice but to fight that war with the "kids" coming out of our high schools and colleges. They are very different from the Greatest Generation, whose soldiers took the fight across France to the Third Reich and whose marines island-hopped across the Pacific to imperial Japan—different generation, different culture. They are different from those of my generation who fought in Vietnam, although the nature of the intractable insurgent enemy I fought in the Mekong Delta is not dissimilar to the insurgents in Mosul.

As a general statement, the current generation of warriors is being asked to fight a difficult, asymmetrical war with unprecedented scrutiny of their conduct, and they come from a culture that may not have prepared them for the moral implications of their conduct on this battlefield. That said, they indeed may very well be the *best generation* we've ever put in the field. The warriors of our all-volunteer force now train to a professional military standard that the Greatest Generation and those of my era never imagined. They certainly enjoy a technical advantage not seen since the British used Martini-Henry rifles and Gatling guns against Zulus armed with spears in the Anglo-Zulu War of 1879. Our guys are *good*. But while their combat capabilities and military skills, when compared to past generations, may be highly advanced, the ethical climate and moral culture that formed them may not have kept pace—and in fact may be a hindrance. In his fine book *Making the Corps*, Thomas Ricks wrote about the "widening gap between military and society." To again go a step further, I would say that the gap between ethical conduct accepted in our civil society and that needed by our warriors on the current battlefield is Grand Canyon-esque—and growing. This may be especially true of the target demographic of our military recruiting efforts—eighteen- to twenty-eight-year-old males.

The all-volunteer force has both advantages and liabilities. With enough volunteers, you can select from a talent pool that can be molded into an effective force with enough "cream" floating to the top to build a leadership cadre for a professional standing force. But as a division officer aboard the USS *Nimitz* said of his sailors in a recent History channel series, "I don't get too many high school valedictorians." We are an affluent society; most young Americans have other options. Yet amid this affluence, many of our volunteers enlist because they have social, economic, or family issues they are trying to put behind them. Many have no other prospects than a tour in the military—for job skills, if nothing else. Others enlist for some nebulous, macho idea of what it is to be a warrior. Still, the generation now joining the military, in one way or another, seeks to serve their nation. More than a few bring a great deal of aptitude for becoming professional warriors, along with genuine patriotic virtue. Yet they have to be trained—physically, professionally, and morally. We seem to accomplish the first two of these requirements well, but the moral and ethical component of our warrior training needs attention.

Only a few years ago I was speaking with a senior SEAL officer about the existing moral condition of our deploying SEAL units. At the time, he had recently finished a tour as commanding officer of a SEAL team and was assigned the task of reviewing the ethical needs of the Naval Special Warfare community; he was the point man for inventorying the moral health of our SEAL warriors. "Dick," he told me, "it's really not that hard. My father and my uncles taught me the difference between right and wrong. It's something that you learn growing up or you don't." I was to later learn that this reflected much of the thinking in our special operations community—ethics based on a predisposition. Since then, the SEALs have made some improvements, adopting an articulated code and ethos and instituting a more robust moral component to basic training, but there's still room for more. Codes and a collective ethos (see Appendixes II and III) are fine, but unless they become part of *the culture*, they're just words on a plaque at the front entrance to the unit. Despite the recent attention given to statements about the concept of ethical warriorship, one fact remains: when taken as a percentage of total training time, a shockingly small amount of time is devoted to the moral conditioning of our warriors—smaller still when taken in the context of operations in an insurgent battlespace and the requirements of counterinsurgency warfare.

In classical ethical training, two questions are asked: *What is right?* and *How do we choose?* What is right (and wrong) behavior on the battlefield is often guided by the rules of engagement—the ROEs. But these rules are guidelines and don't address every situation. The "How do we choose?" part is even more difficult. To be sure, we are not trying to take riflemen and SAW gunners and turn them into classical ethicists, but along with the ROEs, we need to give them better tools to make these kinds of decisions—the ones they make daily in the field. Training time is dear in both our conventional and special operations training pipelines. Yet it would stand to reason that if we cannot allocate more time for ethical training per se, we should make every effort to use that time wisely. Part of this education is not only about how to distinguish between right and wrong conduct in the battlespace, but also about how to make good decisions in a dynamic, asymmetrical environment. Past that there is the important cultural issue of what a warrior will and will not tolerate in his presence—in his squad and in his platoon.

Most of the current training is in the lecture-style-classroom format, with most of the communication going one way—the instructor holding forth and the students listening. This is the *least* effective way to teach battlefield conduct (or anything else, for that matter). We need more interactive and Socratic methods to bring this important information across to our warriors. Most of what passes for ethical warriorship training takes place during basic and initial advanced training; too little is done after these young warriors leave the womb of the training command. We need to look at changing this practice. Effective ethical training and moral grounding for our warriors has to be ongoing and integrated with tactical considerations and the operational environment. What is learned in training has to be reinforced in the operational components.

There are various subsets within what has come to be called the military culture. There is the culture in the training commands, which is very formatted and controlled. Then there is the domestic, garrison culture, in which the warriors serve almost on a part-time basis; they spend time with their unit and time away from the unit, with family and friends—time away from the military setting. Then there is the deployed culture—and all too often this is a very distinct and permissive culture. Here the phrase "what happens on deployment, stays on deployment" applies, and that's not always good. Our training commands are very good at teaching physical and professional skill sets to our warriors. In many cases they don't do a bad job with the moral skill set. But at the level of the operational units, things can change. Typically the new men want to be accepted in the unit and be a part of the operational warrior culture. This need to belong is powerful—it's why many of these men volunteered. The new men will do almost anything to conform to the operational culture—including engaging in wrong behavior. This is why moral conditioning and ethos-based training and awareness are so important in garrison, during predeployment training, and in the deployed tactical units. Right conduct and intolerance of wrong conduct must be continually reinforced.

The goal here, and it's not an easy one, is to challenge warriors, men new to the ranks and veterans alike, to take ownership of the moral health of their units—to cover each other in matters of honor and right conduct, just as they do tactically on patrol. These ideas can be introduced in the classroom, but classes in ethics and moral grounding alone can be difficult, even counterproductive; our warriors are doers—people of action. While some issues will have to be addressed in the classroom, an *integration* of tactical training and ethical training/awareness is also needed.

In later chapters I will refer often to the work being done at the Close Quarters Defense Academy and of the awareness and sustainment training in the Marine Corps. Both have done some interesting work in blending the tactical and the ethical. I will also talk about the physical and professional side of military training as those skill sets relate to warrior ethical conditioning. In many cases I will cite examples from Navy SEAL and Army Special Forces training, since my recent experience and writing have addressed these training pipelines. Both of these SOF venues may prove instructional because few of our nation's warriors are better trained for combat, nor do any ground-combat units, to my knowledge, have more distinct and entrenched cultures.

In many ways, we are not just the sole superpower; we are also a warrior nation. We have an admirable and noble warrior culture. As we begin this study, let's first take a look at some of the historical forces that brought our warrior culture to this point in time.

CHAPTER TWO

Conflict and Conduct

The notion of competition, conflict, and war goes back well before recorded history. Extended families, tribes, and clans have long used violence to acquire—at the expense of neighboring families, tribes, and clans—food, water, or shelter. The great city-states of Athens and Sparta competed for resources, influence, and treasury. Armies, and then navies, grew, and with that growth there came a greater influence of the military class within those societies. Standing armies became commonplace, along with the professional development and an improved social standing of the warrior. The Crusades and the Islamic jihad ushered in wars and campaigns of conquest carried out for religious purposes; these wars were fought for the extension of faith or the defense of it. The rise of nation-states brought national boundaries and international recognition of sovereignty. The Peace of Westphalia in 1648 ended the Thirty Years War. With the signing of that treaty, religion ceased to be a major cause for war, at least in Europe. The major nation-states decided that what went on within the boundaries of a nation was the business of that nation, and civil wars were internal affairs. The conduct of war became a nation-to-nation endeavor, and humankind began the era during which wars were fought between sovereign nations or alliances of sovereigns. And warriors, who now pledged their allegiance to the state, took on added dimension and stature within the nations for whose cause they fought. The eighteenth and nineteenth centuries witnessed wars of aggression, conquest, and revolution (including our own), as well as civil wars (including our own). With each passing decade, new technologies led to new weaponry, and new tactics led to the more sophisticated application of force. Standing armies grew larger, more mobile, and more lethal.

The last century ushered in the first of the world wars and began the bloodiest century known to man. By some accounts close to a hundred million people perished in war, or as collateral damage of war, in the twentieth century. By midcentury the advent of nuclear weapons had made full-on, large-scale war between nations unthinkable, or at least far less likely. Long term, however, the development of such weapons has done little to prevent the small and medium-sized wars that quickly became modern surrogates for nationalism and competition.

As of this writing, the United States is straining under its commitments in the Middle East and Southwest Asia, even as a resurgent Russia is beginning to flex its muscles in the former Soviet republics and the economic engine that is modern China continues to gather momentum. The Russian army that stormed into Georgia in 2008 was a different force than the one that left Afghanistan with its tail between its legs in 1989. For China, the need for oil and resources will surely lead to an expansion of its military capabilities. As for the new Russia, it has vast reserves of oil and natural gas. These resources will fund that nation's military expansion and serve as economic leverage over eastern and western Europe. Only a few years ago, the United States stood alone as the sole superpower, militarily and economically. Those days may be coming to an end. We may yet function as the world's policeman, but it seems as if there may be some new and potentially thuggish actors in the mix.

Still, America holds more than a few cards in this global poker game. Militarily we possess a very experienced and seasoned force—one that is currently, and for the foreseeable future, without peer. Since 9/11, we've developed a far more proficient force. Stepping past the contentious issues of invasion, the aftermath of invasion, and the public and political disillusionment about our ventures in Iraq and Afghanistan, along with the soaring costs, our nation currently enjoys a capable and highly professional military. That force is evolving away from the traditional role of defeating national armies and navies to one that serves in the role of global policeman, inasmuch as we wish to continue in that role. At the expense of its capability in maneuver warfare and strategic deterrent, our military is moving to expand its ability to contend in small wars and regional insurgent conflicts. This development has not come about without some controversy. For some time there has been much debate about this, along with a not-so-small pushback from conventional military thinkers. How much attention and treasury do we allocate away from the traditional roles of airpower, sea power, and land-based conventional muscle (nuclear ships, long-range delivery platforms, space-based technologies, and armored divisions) to the business at hand—insurgency warfare in Iraq and Afghanistan? I think it's safe to say that we will have to remain aware and be prepared to engage in large-scale military operations, but that our most probable future engagements will look a lot more like Iraq and Afghanistan than World War II or Korea. Who knows what our armed forces may be asked to do as we move into the second decade of the twenty-first century—perhaps play a counterinsurgency role in Pakistan or carry out a Soviet-style regional containment of Iran?

Currently we call our enemies terrorists; in reality they are Islamic extremists. Terrorists thrive in insurgent conditions, and insurgencies are difficult business; they require a very special military and paramilitary skill set. Furthermore, the expertise and ground-force composition devoted to this kind of warfare may be of limited use in countering the growing military influence of Russia and China. And while our Islamist enemies, allied with al-Qaeda, challenge us with low-tech, insurgent tactics and terrorism, their global strategy is most sophisticated, as the 2008 attack on Mumbai would suggest. These people are not to be underestimated.

Yet I find it fascinating that not all aspects of our military have experienced change. Amid all the transformation and innovation brought on by technology and global military requirements, we still cling to the traditional, sometimes ancient, and even noble notions of what a warrior is and what we expect of warrior conduct on the battlefield. And this plunges us into tactical ethics. For all the talk of emerging global threats, shifting regional alliances, and non-state actors, the tactical rubber still meets the military road when a deployed squad or platoon steps onto the battleground. If our national interests require that we put these boots on the ground, then it's the warriors who are asked to conduct ground-warfare operations who matter. It's important that we understand this world from their perspective—what the Army often calls "ground truth."

The persona of the warrior has changed surprisingly little over time, though there have been some refinements in and codification of warrior conduct. This is particularly the case when compared with the dramatic changes in the technology and methodologies of warfare. The warrior persona is a very singular and individual concept. Throughout recorded history, the notion and character of a warrior has been a compelling issue, often historically more meaningful than the battle or the cause. For much of his evolution, the term "warrior" has been synonymous with "hero." Tales extolling the warrior's virtue, courage, and heroic conduct were probably told around campfires long before we began to write down these exploits. The most notable of the ancient warriors were the Homeric heroes of *The Iliad* and *The Odyssey*—Hector, Achilles, and Odysseus. While Homer's works are considered fiction, there is much debate about the real men who defended Troy and those who sacked it. What is clear is that proficient and noble conduct of warriors on the battlefield curried favor with the citizenry and with the gods, while cowardice and weakness were held in contempt. Men were clearly preeminent on the battlefield, but warrior virtues were assigned to both women and men. We revere the Spartan mother who told her son to come home with his shield or on it. To abandon your shield and come home without it meant that you broke ranks and ran—the conduct of a coward. Wounded or slain Spartan warriors were carried home on their shields with honor. The notion of battlefield honor, accolades for courage and success in battle, and spoils awarded to the victors can be traced back three millennium.

The journey of the warrior since the time of Homer has followed parallel tracks of favor and necessity. As nations embarked on war, they in many ways ritualized warfare as they sought to champion those who fought. Those who fought well brought tribute and honor to their nations. The Roman Empire was sometimes led by hedonists, but often by bold and competent generals. A proven warrior leader or field commander was often a national leader, both in the Western nations and those in Asia and the Middle East—men like Leonidas, Alexander, Genghis Khan, Napoléon, and Washington. In tribal societies, such as the Plains Indians, the best and bravest warrior was often the tribal leader. Even into present times, a successful military leader is presumed to have some abilities in governance. There have also been warriors in the collective that we respect and admire, such as the Spartans, the samurai, the Nez Percé, and the Shaolin monks. But it's the individual warrior whose ideals and influence are perhaps most felt and have had the greatest impact on today's generation of warriors. In America, these are men like Robert Rogers, Nathanael Greene, Jim Bowie, Crazy Horse, Alvin York, Audie Murphy, L. B. "Chesty" Puller, and William Darby. We admire them, and our young warriors study and emulate them. Those who demonstrate courage and virtue in combat are given medals and recognition; they enjoy position and prestige in our culture. Even those who oppose war will more often than not honor the warriors in their society.

On the other side of the equation is the perception of the warrior as a threat or a destroyer. That notion is certainly a factor in competing societies and in those that suffer defeat or occupation by foreign warriors. While war and conquest have had their hand in the spread of cultures and ideas, a great deal of suffering, misery, and humiliation has come from war and the aftermath of war, often in the pillage and exploitation of the losing side by the winner. The disruption and destruction caused by warriors in victory, and even by defeated warriors in retreat, have led to some of history's greatest tragedies. Examples include the scourges of Genghis Khan, the rape of Nanking, and our own treatment of the Plains Indians—the latter not being one of our nation's best moments. Yet history has usually condemned wrong warrior behavior, even when it is an isolated incident and even in light of more egregious behavior on the part of the enemy. There has emerged over time some idea or common expectation of what is acceptable and unacceptable in the way of battlefield conduct. At the tactical level, even in the midst of the most vicious combat, it has long been the custom, if not always observed, of giving quarter to an enemy who yields. The mutilation or desecration of the corpse of a fallen enemy is scorned, especially in the cool aftermath of battle. Right treatment of civilians and noncombatants has often been observed by conquering armies, but not always. Many ancient armies laid waste to conquered cities, slaughtering and enslaving noncombatants. But this is not only an ancient concept. In World War II, cities and civilians became targets of warfare—even nuclear warfare. Certainly our current insurgent enemies see cities and civilians as legitimate targets, and even consider the harming of friendly populations as justifiable collateral damage.

Excepting plague and climate-altering events, war is clearly the most destructive element in the history of humankind. Few civilizations have not been touched by war, or not felt the extended effects of war. Such effects are usually negative. These could range from the loss of a friend or loved one to being irritated by the coverage of war on the nightly news to believing that funds used for war could be better spent here at home. Yet amid the suffering and cultural disruption caused by war, our warriors are still honored, and the right conduct of war is regarded as virtuous. On the issue of trust, our military stands foremost in the eyes of Americans—as the following graph illustrates.

It's not surprising that over the centuries, among those who practice war and fight under a national banner, there has evolved a code of sorts—the code of the warrior. In the American experience, this notion of honor on the battlefield was brought from Europe to the colonies and surfaced in 1776 during the War of Independence. It continued into the Civil War; even in that bitter struggle, there was

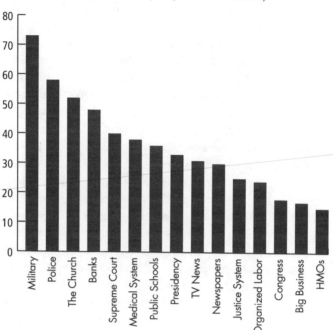

Fig. 1 **AMERICA'S CONFIDENCE** (Gallup Poll June 1–4 2006)

humane conduct and acts of chivalry. On an individual level, soldiers would cross skirmish lines to trade coffee for tobacco. Both sides stood down to permit the clearing of dead and wounded from the battlefield between engagements. Ulysses S. Grant allowed the men in Robert E. Lee's army to return home with their rifles and their mules. In one of the more poignant demonstrations of respect of that war, Union general Joshua Chamberlain ordered his men to attention and to "carry arms" as the defeated Confederate soldiers paraded past. This largely implicit code was set down in rules, and at least in part, by Union army General Orders No. 100 in 1863, which established regulations for the treatment of civilians and POWs. Regarding the latter, neither side, be it at Andersonville or Camp Douglas, treated enemy prisoners as humanely as it might have. American conduct in war was further codified by the U.S. Army's

Rules of Land Warfare in 1914. This document and subsequent updates, which include a 130-page revision in 1940, have guided our conduct in battle through two world wars and many smaller ones, including those being fought today. The Rules of Land Warfare are American and dictate unilateral conduct. The Geneva Conventions of 1949 set standards for international conduct, primarily regarding the treatment of noncombatants and POWs. The Geneva Conventions are recognized by just under two hundred nations.

Warrior codes both empower and restrain the warrior. This is especially true in America, where our Constitution provides for civilian control of our military. Constitutional issues aside, there has evolved within most societies and warrior cultures some notion of right and wrong conduct in war. These constraints or virtues seem to parallel those societal virtues expressed by natural law theorists—those who champion reason as a guide to moral and ethical conduct. This has led to a social contract of sorts between the warrior and his society, and the expectations of his conduct, both in war and in peace—over there and back here at home. The contract is the basis of a code that determines what society expects of its warriors; if a warrior meets those expectations, he will be valued and honored by the society he serves. There have been many written works on warrior codes and published doctrine that govern warrior conduct. I'm always surprised and more than a little gratified when our corporate warriors, finding themselves exceeding their ethical boundaries or needing some self-imposed restraint, turn to the military for assistance and moral recalibration.

There is another code—a code within a code, if you will—as to how the *warrior culture* conducts itself. *This* code relates specifically to how warriors view and treat each other, and their collective conduct as they prosecute war. There have been instances in which warrior and societal codes merge, as in ancient Sparta or among the Mongols whose rolling warrior culture pushed across Asia to eastern Europe and into the Middle East. But for the most part, warriors fight for their clan, tribe, or nation, to defend or expand it, and when the fighting is done, they repatriate themselves back into their societies. The relationship of the warrior to his people—the us and the them—is important, for it defines how people view their warriors and how the warrior sees himself through the eyes of his people. In America we've been historically fascinated with the idea of the citizen soldier and of a small standing army that can be expanded when needed—plowshares to swords and back again. That has been our heritage. I'm not sure how valid that is today with an all-volunteer force, or even how valid it has been since World War II, given the large standing professional military cadre we've had in place since then. Still, this integration of citizenry and soldiering makes for a blending of the civilian and military cultures, which we will later explore in some detail.

Yet there is distinction and segregation when citizens become warriors. To the point of this book, I believe the citizen soldier, or at least the idea of the citizen soldier, loses some civility at the pointy end of the spear—that is, at the tactical level, with small units fighting in close combat for extended periods of time. I further believe that during mortal combat, a warrior's conduct depends on small-unit ethos and the influence of the fellow fighting next to him. There are other factors, but this one counts for a great deal. The "external" controls, the rules imposed by society and the conventions of warfare, lose influence with time and distance. Four soldiers in a Humvee on patrol near Kandahar share a bond and are more important to each other than anything that may have come down from the colonel or the Constitution, or can be imposed by any set of rules. Their situation and their mutual requirements in combat may put the needs of their fellow soldier ahead of their command, their god, their nation, and their family—that family which is safe at home. At that moment in time, those four soldiers in the Humvee *are* family. Warrior codes, both expressed and implied, have value in conditioning our warriors, but it's my contention that we should focus on the cultural implications of our warrior code and how that code relates to the small-unit culture, both in garrison and in tactical situations.

Yet another way to look at this is in terms of hierarchies that affect and influence a young warrior. First, there is the individual soldier—in the field or on patrol, in garrison, or at home with his family and friends. This is a bottom-up hierarchy. What does he think is important? What does he value most in terms of an ethos that will serve his interests and guide his actions in battle? What will allow him to project his force professionally and effectively, and what will encourage him to use restraint when needed? And what will keep him and his buddies safe? In short, what does that Marine lance corporal or Army specialist admire and value most? I've spoken to many soldiers, marines, and special operators, and their collective, individual hierarchies favor the individual warrior—the individual *contemporary* warrior. Who in *their* unit is good on patrol? Who can be counted on in a firefight? Who has tactical savvy and good judgment in combat? That "alpha male" may be the lieutenant or the sergeant, or it may be a veteran fellow soldier with good professional military skills. Not all combat leaders have bars on their collars or chevrons on their sleeves. This is not surprising. Skillful warriors have great value and influence, which is not surprising. Our soldiers have been weaned on the exploits of warriors past.

They admire warrior bands and cultures, from the Spartans at Thermopylae to the Band of Brothers in France, but they *really* admire King Leonidas and Major Dick Winters. The German commandos were arguably the best of the Wehrmacht, yet when we study them we study individual warriors like Otto Skorzeny, who parachuted into the Alps in 1943 to save Benito Mussolini and keep Italy in the war on the side of the Axis. There is little we now study about Italian military operations in World War II save for the intrepidity of the Italian frogmen. Six of these brave combat swimmers sank the British battleship *Queen Elizabeth* in Alexandria Harbor in 1941. In the context of our elite warriors, one has only to visit the Army's JFK Special Warfare Center and School at Fort Bragg. Near the main entrance is a hall dedicated to the twenty-one Special Forces soldiers awarded the Medal of Honor. The Navy SEALs afford much the same honor to their five Medal of Honor recipients, two of them so honored since 9/11. This measure of individual honor and respect extends collectively to fallen warriors. At the deployed home of the 1st Armored Division in Stuttgart, Germany, whose 1st Brigade elements fought in the Battle of Ramadi, there is a manicured field with rows of planted trees, one for each member of the division killed in battle in Iraq and Afghanistan. Two of those trees bear the names of Navy SEALs killed fighting alongside 1st Brigade soldiers in Ramadi. The respect afforded battlefield bravery and our fallen warriors is a powerful force in our culture at large; Arlington National Cemetery is one of our most revered memorials. Within the military, these traditions of valuing individual courage in combat and honoring our fallen warriors are highly amplified and become incrementally more influential in the smaller combat units.

I've previously mentioned that Warrant Officer Hugh Thompson, the helicopter pilot who risked his life and that of his crew at My Lai to try to stop the slaughter, was shunned by his colleagues after the incident; they treated him like a traitor. It took the military thirty years to recognize his gallantry during that shameful incident. Yet you will find few of our warriors today who recognize the name of Hugh Thompson or understand his gallantry. This is an important clue to a little-understood aspect of our warrior culture—and perhaps a flaw in our public (media-driven?) perception of a warrior. It is the imbalance of what we value as courage and choose to ignore in the way of compassion.

Then there is the top-down hierarchy that governs acceptable conduct in war. This has been codified over the years, but most often cited in the Geneva Conventions of 1949. This is the document that the warring parties signed coming out of World War II, and it remains the standard for American forces engaged in combat around the world. Because the United States is a signatory to these conventions, they carry the weight of the Constitution as they are imposed on our military in combat. These conditions and restrictions are further refined by theater- and area-specific rules of engagement—the all-important ROEs—but the local rules will in no way violate those put in place by the Geneva Conventions.

In conventional war, these rules work pretty well. In conventional war, the objectives are to destroy, isolate, neutralize, or restrict the movement of enemy forces, and to take ground. The ROEs associated with this kind of combat flow from our adherence to international conventions and our own humane intentions—those formed from within our culture of restraint, as well as from the idea that we should treat the enemy with decency, on the battlefield or as a prisoner of war, because that is how we want our soldiers treated. These same constraints apply to nonmilitary targets and civilian noncombatants. However, it has to be noted that deviation from these rules, in the heat of battle or in those isolated incidents of willful misconduct that seem to plague all wars, do not affect the outcome of conventional battle. Such violations of right conduct are usually dealt with in the aftermath of war, as lessons learned or in war-crimes proceedings. In short, the typical response to improper battlespace conduct seems to be that it happens. That's regrettable, and not in keeping with the right conduct of most of our troops. To one degree or another, most conventional enemy combatants hold at least some of these ideas about right conduct, though their view of the matter may be colored by their nationality or other considerations. Furthermore, both sides in a conventional war are more than aware of the perception of wrong conduct in the light of world opinion. This has never been more the case than with the modern battlefield, which is highly transparent. So for any number of reasons, military operations in conventional war are well served by the Geneva Conventions and an internationally perceived standard of right conduct. From a utilitarian perspective, it's simply in the interest of conventional combatants to play by the rules.

Additionally, conventional warfare lends itself to the more familiar and traditional command and control of engaged forces. While much of the actual fighting is done at the squad and platoon level, those ground-combat elements are in close communication with their company, battalion, and regimental commanders. Major advancing and maneuvering elements, the battalions and regiments, are set pieces on the field of battle, and senior leaders are seldom isolated from those fighting on the front. Down the chain of command, a company-level commander is never too distant from his troops or his battalion organization. Those engaged in conventional war may experience periods of time-distance communication disruption as elements surge and maneuver, but there are often pauses in the action that allow for the re-formation and consolidation of command. This process keeps engaged units in touch with the chain of command, permitting an ongoing enforcement of the rules of engagement. A platoon or company commander can usually pick up the radio and check in with "higher" and get direction. And as we saw in the push into Kuwait in 1991 and the drive toward Baghdad in 2003, large-scale, mechanized, air-supported campaigns are relatively short in duration.

This is not always the case on the insurgent battlefield. The notions of right and wrong conduct and a strict battlefield ethos don't play out so nicely. The rules, at least for us, are the same, but the application is far more difficult. As previously mentioned (and probably not for the last time), insurgencies are a battle for the people. The insurgent enemy hides within the local population, which does two things for him. It causes the counterinsurgent force, which has been largely America's role since 9/11, to fight an enemy who is sometimes indistinguishable from the population that is the object of battle. This means it is very easy for us to get a bad result, even when we are tactically successful in engaging the insurgents. There is the ever-present possibility of collateral damage, even as our troops may be assuming additional risk in consideration of noncombatant safety. Second, an insurgent enemy hiding among the people has a far more intimate knowledge of the battlespace. He can recruit from the people, they are his source of logistics and intelligence, and they afford cover and concealment. More important, he can influence and intimidate them; the people may willingly yield to the needs of the insurgent, or they may be coerced. This gives the insurgent leverage and control. *He* has a relationship and a permanence with the locals that is far more difficult for *us* to achieve.

Quite often we feel that our genuine concern for a contested population should count for something in an insurgency—that our restraint and our ideals and our compassion should give us some traction in the battle. Sometimes they do, but in a war for the hearts and minds of the people, we often don't control the agenda or the perceptions of our actions. And the insurgents are not always uncaring of the people. Hezbollah owes much of its success and popularity to its, for lack of a better term, community outreach. When it's a battle for the people, perceptions are important. So is security. Very little takes place in a community if there is no security. It is the primary job of both elected leaders and tribal leaders to keep the peace—to protect the people. It's also the element of community life that is most easily disrupted by insurgent forces. When we get involved, *our* primary objective is security—providing it ourselves, or assisting the local police or military in providing it. If security is not achieved, then we and the local police lose. The insurgents don't necessarily win, but then neither do we. Underlying all this is the sure notion on the part of the people *and* the local police that the insurgents will be there indefinitely; we will not. Advantage, insurgents.

There is also a difference in the application of the rules that govern war in an insurgent environment. In conventional war, it's a top-down application of the rules of engagement, with the more-senior command-and-control elements governing battlefield conduct. I'll make the case that in an insurgency the imposed rules, at least on our side, may be a top-down mandate but that the application is bottom up. The generals look to their brigade commanders, the colonels, for ROE compliance, and the colonels put this same responsibility on their battalion commanders—the lieutenant colonels. From the battalion level, the torch gets passed to the company commanders and component task unit commanders. It's there—at the company/task unit level—that we win or lose insurgent wars; that's where the key combat leaders are. These Army and Marine captains and majors are the warrior leaders that get it done or don't get it done in an insurgency. They are the direct supervisors of the platoons and squads that carry the fight to the enemy in Iraq and Afghanistan. More important, it is the conduct of their men in the field that shapes the battle for the hearts and minds of the people.

In short, how these men act is everything. And it's their job to know if their lieutenants and senior noncommissioned officers (NCOs) are conducting operations within the rules of engagement or not. But the question of right conduct in the insurgent battlespace goes well beyond ROE compliance. Killing an "insurgent" in a given situation may be legal, but is it moral from the perspective of those around him? Does the taking of that life contribute to winning the battle—that is, to winning the people? Collectively these decisions are mission critical. That's why we need our very best warriors in those important junior-officer and senior-NCO positions.

The division between the battalion and the company-level grade is more than a senior-junior command issue; it has broader implications. I've heard company and task unit commanders say more than once, "Those guys at battalion really don't know what the hell we're up against out here." That makes sense for several reasons. With each passing year since 9/11 and each passing combat rotation for our combat leaders, they become more experienced and more aware of what's happening in their battlespace. Early on, everyone was new to the business of ongoing, continuous combat operations, and, more specifically, operations in an insurgent environment. That's no longer the case, because we've been at this going on nine years, but direct combat experience only goes up the line so far. Very few of the battalion commanders are veterans of small-unit combat simply because they were too senior to serve as platoon leaders when we began ground actions in Iraq and Afghanistan. Some may have been small-unit leaders in the First Gulf War, but that was maneuver warfare, not sustained counterinsurgency warfare. This is not the case for the captains and majors. Most of them have commanded in combat, and they *know* what their troops are going through; they've been there recently, and often. And it's not unusual for the captain or the major to occasionally go on patrol or to work directly with his Iraqi or Afghan counterpart in the field. That doesn't happen as often with the battalion commanders; neither they nor their opposite numbers in the Iraqi or Afghan security forces spend a great deal of time in the field. It's simply not their job. Experience aside, the responsibilities at battalion are different than at the company level. By its nature, the work of counterinsurgency is a small-unit undertaking. So what happens in the field is in the hands of the junior officers and senior noncoms.

There's little value, at least in this work, in addressing the disappointing results and missed opportunities following the 2003 invasion of Iraq to blunt the insurgency that followed. So I'm going to fast-forward to when General David Petraeus stepped onto the scene as Commander, Multi-National Force–Iraq in January 2007, and we began to get it right. The getting it right was not so much a new or revolutionary tactical innovation as it was the application of existing counterinsurgency (COIN) doctrine. It just took a man of Petraeus' stature and vision to bend our conventional forces into accepting and applying the proven COIN measures. When we began to realize that the battle was not *against* al-Qaeda or the insurgents but rather *for* the people, we began to win in Iraq. Afghanistan is a different set of problems, but the war there is still insurgency warfare—still a battle for the human terrain, and, I might add, very difficult human terrain.

General Petraeus moved us through the difficult and hard-to-measure steps of indigenous-force training, civil-affairs projects, tribal engagement, reconstruction, and local political engagement. Few of our commanders at the brigade and division level were trained to do this. Few of them wanted to do this; they and their subordinates at the battalion and even the company level wanted to fight insurgents. The soldiers and marines in the platoons and squads wanted to fight insurgents. It's the mission they train for. In the case of many of our warriors, it's why they volunteered. Surprisingly, I also found this to be the case within our special operations components. Without question, kinetic, direct-action operations are something we are very good at. Unfortunately, these skills are of limited and selective value in winning an insurgency. An insurgency is a tyranny of the minority, and insurgent foot soldiers are a renewable resource. The killing of insurgents has its place, but in the long run, we don't *win* insurgencies. Let me say this again: *we don't win insurgencies.* We win the people, and the people defeat the insurgents. Imagine! Now, we have a role to play in this, and the people may not be able to do it without us. Our role may call on us to use our technology and our professional use of arms, but it remains that *they* have to do it; we can only help. We can thank David Petraeus for the shift in tactical thinking and local engagement that turned things around and gave us some hope for success in Iraq.

If our recent ventures in the Middle East and Southwest Asia have taught us one thing, it's that our time—in Iraq, Afghanistan, or any of these places—is limited. So it's not how good we are that's important, nor is it how many insurgents we may have killed; it's how well we can train *the locals* before we have to leave. We *will* leave, and then it will be up to them. We may have a long and even open-ended role that involves training, combat support, medical support, intelligence, and logistics, and perhaps even a stay-behind role for a small special-missions presence to deal with an occasional high-value target. But when we invade, we must be seen to leave. At some point, Americans in Humvees should not be patrolling the countryside or rumbling through villages.

As we move on to a discussion on just how we train our warriors, and a focus on what they will need to know to fight on the insurgent battlefield, it's helpful to understand not only the capabilities of our ground-combat elements, but their limitations as well. We also need to understand that the days of our going to war and winning the physical terrain as a path to victory are over. And winning over the people is only a part of the mission—maybe the easy part. The harder and more telling elements are the conditions and the capability of the local security forces we leave behind.

CHAPTER THREE

Warriorship 101

I have a friend who is a noted Hollywood movie producer. He grew up in Germany and came to the United States when he was in his late teens. His European upbringing and his movie-making profession give him a unique perspective on our (now his) culture and our military.

"I'm continually fascinated by the relationship of America to her military forces and their role in American society," he told me. "Things are different in Germany and, to an extent, all of Europe. I can't remember singing our national anthem at a sporting event, let alone saying a pledge of allegiance in school. There's no such thing as a military color guard or a posting of the colors at a sporting event, nor any reference or reverence for the flag, nor any mention of those who may have served. My German generation is essentially one of patriotic eunuchs. Our relationship to our nation, our flag, and our military is nothing like it is here. What goes on in America is unique, and I find it very compelling."

For a relatively young nation, America indeed has a long and rich military tradition. For a nation of immigrants who imported their initial traditions, we have evolved in a way that is uniquely . . . well, uniquely American. This includes the role of the warrior in our society, and the value and perception the American people have of their warriors. Even as our culture has moved in ways that are progressive, entrepreneurial, commercial, self-serving, and even hedonistic, we have expectations that our military will somehow be above all that. In many ways, we expect our military and our warriors to be *better* than ourselves. Furthermore, I think our military calls on itself to represent the best of American society, as if in some way they are the guardians of our values as well as our borders. I don't think this is a bad bargain between the warrior and his people, but it does create some problems. It means that when a young American decides to become an American warrior, some changes may have to take place—in some cases, dramatic changes. There is a Rubicon of sorts that has to be crossed.

Even as our current service composition and deployment postures are bound by tradition, so is the training we give our new warriors. This formal military training is some of the best and most refined in the world. It still begins with basic training—the training that takes American civilians and turns them into American warriors. For the purposes of this book, I'm going to focus on the basic training of those preparing for ground combat, specifically the infantry training of soldiers and marines and the training/advanced training of selected special operations components. Furthermore, I will concentrate on the training of male soldiers, marines, and special operators, as ground-combat operations performed by our armed forces remain a male-only business. Let's begin with the Marines.

Perhaps no other organization in our military, or any military, takes basic training as seriously as the United States Marine Corps. And few organizations, military or otherwise, are as tradition bound or proud of their heritage as the Marines. I make the following statement with respect and admiration: the Marine Corps embodies the characteristics of a fraternal order, a club, and a cult. Yet this force is not exclusive. The Corps extends an open invitation to a wide range of young Americans to join its ranks. All a person has to do is pass the entrance screening and submit him- or herself to the rigors of Marine basic training. Like all the services, current needs have caused the Corps to adjust its recruiting standards and approach in accordance with the existing societal norms to achieve its recruiting quotas and service requirements. And, like all services, the quantity and quality of recruits may depend on economic conditions in the United States and the level of active employment of our forces. Yet the Marine Corps always seems to ramp up and modernize its basic training to mold its recruits into good marines. What makes for a good marine today is essentially what has made for a good marine for a very long time, and the Marine Corps is slightly older than our nation itself. Since this book deals with the warrior ethos, I'm going to further narrow our focus on the moral and ethical components of Marine Corps basic training.

The Marines train their recruits at Paris Island, South Carolina, and San Diego, California. The Corps conducts a twelve-week intensive training regime that controls virtually every aspect of the recruit's life. The term "24/7," widely used in the popular lexicon, is, for the most part, merely a figure of speech. This is not the case in Marine basic training—or, for that matter, in any of our service basic-training venues. The Marine Corps oversees the transformation (its term) of some 35,000 young men, as well as 3,000 women, from civilian to marine in one of the most comprehensive and well-choreographed military training evolutions on earth. I've been a student of military training for the past two decades. Nothing, in my opinion, is so dramatic or as "transformational" as Marine Corps basic training, or "entry-level" training, as the Corps refers to it.

The value metric for the Marines, as for the Navy, is Honor, Courage, Commitment. The Marines have a long and storied history, and they use that sense of history to good advantage. New recruits are immediately placed under the obligation of this honorable and celebrated past. And this obligation, in the words of "The Marines' Hymn," is "to keep our honor clean." The Corps' value-based training is an expansion and re-formation of the Honor, Courage, Commitment theme, which forms the basis for the Marine Corps Core Values. These are formally stated here in an excerpt from the Marine Corps Reference Publication 6-11B, *Marine Corps Values: A Users Guide for Discussion Leaders*.

(1) **HONOR**—The Marine Corps is a unique institution, not just to the military, but to the nation and the world. As the guardians of the standards of excellence for our society,

Marines must possess the highest sense of gallantry in serving the United States of America and embody responsibility to duty above self, including, but not limited to:

Integrity, Demonstrating the highest standards of consistent adherence to right, legal and ethical conduct.

Responsibility, Personally accepting the consequences for decisions and actions. Coaching right decisions of subordinates. A chain is only as strong as the weakest individual link, but a battalion of Marines is more like a cable. Together we are stronger than any individual strand, but one strand may hold us together in a crisis if it's strong enough. One Marine taking responsibility for a situation may save the day.

Honesty, Telling the truth. Overt honesty in word and action and clarifying possible misunderstanding or misrepresentation caused by silence or inaction when you should speak up. Respecting other's property and demonstrating fairness in all actions. Marines do not lie, cheat, or steal.

Tradition, Demonstrating respect for the customs, courtesies, and traditions developed over many years for good reason, which produce a common Marine Corps history and identity.

Respect for the heritage and traditions of others, especially those we encounter in duty around the world.

(2) **COURAGE**—Moral, mental, and physical strength to resist opposition, face danger, and endure hardship, including, but not limited to:

Self-Discipline, Marines hold themselves responsible for their own actions and others responsible for their actions. Marines are committed to maintaining physical, moral, and mental health, to fitness and exercise, and to life long learning.

Patriotism, Devotion to and defense of one's country. The freely chosen, informed willingness to support and defend the Constitution of the United States.

Loyalty, Steady reliability to do one's duty in service to the United States of America, the United States Marine Corps, one's command, one's fellow Marines, Sailors, Soldiers, Airmen, citizens, oneself, and to family.

Valor, Boldness and determination in facing danger in battle, and the daily commitment to excellence and honesty in actions small and large.

(3) **COMMITMENT**—The promise or pledge to complete a worthy goal by worthy means which requires identification with that goal and demonstrated actions to support that goal, including, but not limited to:

Competence, Maintaining, and improving one's skill level to support the team. Commitment to growing toward a standard of excellence second to none.

Teamwork, Individual effort in support of other team members in accomplishing the team's mission. Marines take care of their own. All worthwhile accomplishments are the result of a team effort.

Selflessness, Marines take care of their subordinates, their families, their fellow Marines before themselves. The welfare of our country and our Corps is more important than our individual welfare.

Concern for People, The Marine Corps is the custodian of this nation's future, her young people. We exist to defend the nation, but as importantly, we are in the business of creating honorable citizens. Everyone is of value, regardless of race, nation of origin, religion, or gender. Concern includes a commitment to improving the level of education, skill, self-esteem, and quality of life for Marines and their families. On the battlefield, a Marine is the fiercest of all warriors and the most benevolent of conquerors.

Spiritual Heritage, The U.S. Constitution, the Pledge of Allegiance, and the creeds that guide our nation recognize the value of religious and spiritual heritage of individuals and base our understanding of rights and duties on the endowment of all people, by God, with the inalienable rights of life, liberty, and the pursuit of happiness. Marines maintain spiritual health and growth to nurture enduring values and acquire a source of strength required for success in battle and the ability to endure hardship.

This statement of core values is a pretty tall order, for this or any military organization. It's also a very unambiguous standard for what the Marines expect from their new warriors. Within the context of what American civil society might expect of its young adult males, it can call for an enormous personal reorientation. The Marines understand that a great deal of change has to take place for a young American to become a young marine. While the Marines feel that they can teach and exact a value-based standard of their own making, I find it refreshing that they also recognize that their recruits, for better or worse, bring their own set of values with them. Here is another excerpt from the same document: "Marines bring with them when they enter the Corps their own set of Core Values. Personal Core Values are instilled in marines by their parents, families, religious beliefs, schools, peers, and other influences upon their lives. Regardless of background, every marine should understand that being a marine entails embracing and adhering to Marine Corps Core Values."

This basically says that families have rules, and if you are going to be a member of the Marine family, then, no matter where you are coming from, you have to follow our rules. Marine basic training is a carefully integrated indoctrination of professional military skills, physical training, and moral reorientation. Regarding the moral, the Marines have moved away from a pure lecture format to deliver their character and ethos message. Here the key teaching venue is the core-value discussion. These are interactive discussions at the platoon level that make full use of Socratic teaching methods. It takes skill and restraint to teach this way and to guide the discussion along positive lines without preaching. Interactive teaching means asking questions and listening to the student recruit. I can imagine that it was quite a change to get Marine drill instructors to buy into this, yet it is much more conducive to learning than simply lecturing to the student. And it places a heavier burden on the instructor/discussion leader. It's the same method of instruction we use at the Naval Academy in the teaching of ethics. If a discussion instructor is skillful, he can encourage and precipitate a positive agenda, and the students will learn from each other.

Another uniquely Marine approach to values training is the Marine Corps Martial Arts Program. The Marines have, for want of a better term, co-opted the surging interest in mixed martial arts and ultimate-fighting contests for their own ends. This is a martial arts program designed by the Marines to serve the interests of the Corps. It is designed to integrate physical, mental, and character discipline—the latter to encourage and promote the Marine Corps Core Values. The program seeks to redirect the energy of young recruits into areas of positive personal development that are in keeping with a marine's role as a warrior and as a member of society—warriorship and citizenship. I believe this is an important and positive step in extending the value set promoted in basic training to a value set that is useful in the battlespace. It's also worth mentioning here that the Marine Corps Martial Arts Program also serves as a buffer to the growing popularity of ultimate-fighting contests and mixed-martial-arts competitions—sporting events that attract young male audiences but seem to be violence-without-value attractions.

The Marines have elected to use martial arts training as a vehicle or delivery system to promote mental and character discipline. Twenty-eight hours of instruction during basic training is devoted to this martial arts program. All marines in basic training must earn a level of proficiency in the program, and all marines on activity duty are encouraged to continue with the program to attain higher levels of proficiency.

Just how effective is the Marine Corps basic-training process and its goals of value indoctrination and value reorientation? Outwardly, it's dramatic. One has only to see a particularly sullen, recalcitrant young man before beginning this process and compare that "before" individual to the polite and disciplined end result. It truly is a transformation. In addition to the character-related information from the martial arts training, forty-two hours of dedicated training time is allotted to instruction in values and the Marine warrior ethos. There is neither the time nor the need in this work to go further into the mechanics of the making of a marine or the careful imprinting of Marine Corps Core Values on the new recruits. It is simply worth noting that the Corps puts a premium on the moral and ethical health of its new marines and continually refines this process to achieve this goal. It is also worth noting that the Marines see their role as one that goes well past establishing a set of values that serves their Corps; they believe that the marine who graduates from basic training—someone who has undergone this transformation—is a national treasure. I believe they also see their role in this regard as one of conservatorship—that in many respects they are the keepers of *American* values during a time when these values are under siege by popular culture.

Basic training makes the marine, but not the infantryman. From the basic school, the new marine will then attend the School of Infantry at Camp Pendleton, California, or Camp Geiger, Georgia. This fifty-nine-day course of instruction focuses on the weapons and tactics of infantry operations. There may be other formal schools in a young marine's future, but for our purposes here, we'll briefly focus on infantry training. The School of Infantry concentrates on infantry-related skill sets and physical conditioning, but there is time set aside for character-based training. By design, some thirteen hours are allotted to value-based training designed to sustain what the new marines learned during basic training. This training is designed to reinforce the Marine Corps Core Values as well as to instill culture awareness and to provide a background in the rules of engagement, combat stress, proper sexual conduct, substance abuse control, and equal opportunity. It is also designed to bridge the gap between the rigorous core-values imprinting of basic training and those character challenges a new marine may experience in his operational unit.

The School of Infantry does not enforce the 24/7 regime of Marine basic—the infantrymen-in-training have weekends off—but it is still a very intense and formative time. The new marines are still absorbing and digesting just what it is to be a marine. As during basic training, the marine infantry trainees watch their instructors carefully. It would be a mistake to underestimate the role-model effect of these infantry trainers. Learning infantry skills is serious business, and the character and personal values of the training cadre is not lost on their students. So, much of the reinforcement of values covered during basic training is informally buttressed through the mentoring of these instructors. From the School of Infantry, a marine will join his squad, platoon, company, and battalion and begin training for operational duty and deployment. At this juncture in his journey, the newly minted marine infantryman is as well processed and indoctrinated in the core values of the Marine Corps as he is ever likely to become. What lies ahead for our young warrior is the squad/platoon culture and the demands and challenges this close-knit culture will make on him.

Within the United States Army there are two large-scale training pipelines that put young warriors on the ground in defense of our nation. One is called Basic Combat Training (BCT). BCT is a nine-week course that provides the new recruits with the basics of soldiering, including marching, marksmanship, weapons familiarization, communications, and a host of primary military skills. This course is mainly for the new recruits who will be moving on to specialties *other* than the infantry—armor, artillery, air defense, and the like. I mention this here only because many of these soldiers will find themselves on the ground in Iraq or Afghanistan serving in support roles or as dismounted infantry from their armored vehicles. This basic combat course lists a module of training associated with the nine-week BCT that falls under the broad category of "soldierization." The sixty soldierization hours include history, customs, conduct, personnel inspections, and the like. Within this soldierization module, twenty-two hours are dedicated to values and warrior ethos training.

The other Army basic-training venue is known as One Station Unit Training (OSUT; it is sometimes called One Site Unit Training). As the name implies, the new soldier recruits remain at the same site for basic training and infantry training. Here the Army combines basic training and infantry training, and the courses of instruction are run concurrently by the same instructor cadre. BCT makes soldiers out of civilians; OSUT makes soldiers *and* infantrymen out of civilians. OSUT does for the Army what Marine basic training and the School of Infantry do for the Corps. I say this with the caveat that this comparison suits the purpose of this book—both are training grounds for infantry*men* who are destined for ground-combat units. There are those in the Army and the Marine Corps who bristle at the comparison; each feels that their training is unique and even superior. For our discussion here, we will focus on the fourteen-week OSUT process, as OSUT provides the largest increment of our ground-combat personnel. It also produces, both directly and indirectly, the largest increment of soldiers who go on to become Army ground-combat special operators—Rangers and Green Berets.

One Station Unit Training has classes on Army history, customs, and courtesies for the new infantryman trainees, but the service historical imprinting is not so vigorous as it is with the Marine Corps. Values and warrior ethos training begins with an introduction session on day three of OSUT and continues through week nine of the basic curriculum. This instruction takes place on Sundays when not in the field, usually during the initial weeks of training. Sundays are training days. Time is provided in the morning for religious services, and the balance of the day is devoted to training in values and the warrior ethos. Classroom instruction and discussions focus on each of the seven Army Core Values, which the Army holds to be loyalty, duty, respect, selfless service, honor, integrity, and personal courage. The Army approach in value-based training is similar to that of their Marine Corps brothers, in that both use guided discussions and instructor-student interaction as a way of promoting that branch's core values.

These Sunday training venues focus totally on soldier values and warrior ethos. I found that each training company handled the content of this training a little differently, and each seemed to personalize it in their own way. In some cases the training was handled in aggregate, while in others discussion focused on one or more of the Army Core Values. In some training companies these sessions were conducted by the drill sergeants assigned to those companies' group of trainees. In other companies the company commander or the company first (senior) sergeant came in on Sunday to conduct this training. "I try to make the Army Core Values relevant to the new soldier's world—the world as he sees it," one first sergeant told me. "We have to relate this to what is going on today, both on duty, during his off-duty time, and on the battlefield. A soldier has to understand that no matter where he came from, there are certain expectations of his conduct. There are now standards in his life—the same standards that apply to me, to him, and to his fellow soldiers. The Army and his nation now hold him to these standards, and they apply to him in and out of uniform. Every new group of trainees is different, and sometimes we have to change how we approach the training to meet the needs of the group. We don't change the message, just the way we deliver the message. And we stay on point and go over it again and again until each new soldier understands these core values and how they apply to the expected standards of conduct."

Exact training time devoted to values-related training seemed to vary from training company to training company. Somewhere between thirty-five and forty-five hours of formal training time is devoted to Army Core Values training.

Like all military basic training, good values and right conduct are never far from the modules that address physical and professional training. Both the Marines and the Army try in some degree to integrate moral training with the professional and the physical. This is to the good. During the forced marches, calisthenics, unarmed combat, and marksmanship, warriorship and moral values can be addressed informally and reinforced. And the life of a basic-training recruit is highly influenced by the drill sergeant, whom all services wish to be a positive role model for the new men. Both in the Army and the Marines, these trainers serve as mentors, father figures, and the embodiment of a professional standard. These influential senior enlisted leaders also give the new men their first real glimpse of the moral requirements of the military profession.

Getting back to the Army, what happens outside the classroom may be of more importance in molding the moral health of these young infantry trainees. This comes under the heading of "walking-the-walk is far more important than talking-the-talk." For three and half months, these impressionable new soldiers are under the total control of the OSUT cadre. If what they see in these warrior role models is positive in the way of character and personal ethical values, then the moral seeds planted in the classroom have a much better chance of taking root. In speaking with both Army and Marine training cadres, I found that they take their duties as trainers and role models seriously.

During both the Army and the Marine Corps initial training periods, the goal, aside from the military-professional-physical basics, is to give their new soldiers and marines a moral imprint that they can take with them into their operational units and, ultimately, onto the battlefield. These value-based skill sets will be challenged by the culture these new warriors will meet in their operational units and the ambiguities of the insurgent battlespace.

In this discussion of Marine and Army basic/initial training, I have purposely not addressed the training of officers, as their training is separate and distinct from enlisted training in both services. But for the record, both the Army and the Marine Corps put a premium on the training and grooming of their officer corps, and their training is a rigorous blend of the physical, the professional, and the moral. And, as one might expect, there is an intensive leadership component. Not only are these ground-combat commissioned leaders charged with training their troops and leading them in battle, they are also charged with their moral health. This includes responsibility for their conduct before and during battle. They also bear the responsibility of bringing their troops home from the battlespace morally and psychologically intact. Equally as important as officer training is the grooming of senior enlisted leaders. Again, there is not enough time here to go into this subject fully, but the Army and the Marines rely heavily on enlisted leadership. Among their most important leadership training is that which is devoted to the education and development of their noncommissioned officers.

No one in uniform today is immune from the social forces that shape young Americans; all are exposed to values and societal norms that might be incompatible with military service and leadership on the battlefield. And there are certainly cases in which officer and senior enlisted leadership has failed. Yet there is a level of maturity, screening, and training that accompanies officer development, both commissioned and noncommissioned. While I don't wish to minimize the role of leadership nor indemnify these leaders from their moral responsibilities, I believe that from a training perspective, it is the management of the civilian-to-warrior transition of our enlisted soldiers, marines, and special operators that is central to improving battlefield conduct.

Finally, let's consider the values training, or what might be better referred to as an awareness or reinforcement of the warrior ethos, of special operators—our SOF warriors. I use the terms "awareness" and "reinforcement" here because special operations training is not recruit training. Our special operations forces components involved in ground combat can be generally thought of as Army Rangers, Navy SEALs, Army Special Forces (the Green Berets), the Marine Special Operations Command (relatively new), and what is loosely called the special missions units. The operational role and composition of our special missions units are classified; let's just say that they are an important part of our current SOF deployment posture, and that they have a diverse, direct-action portfolio. It's hard to identify a common ethos within our SOF components, as both the individuals and their SOF component have training and administrative ties to their conventional-branch origins. Additionally, each SOF component has its own character and distinct culture. This diversity and the service-specific/SOF-specific statements of values are addressed in Appendixes II and III. While all new SOF warriors have been through their service-branch-specific basic/initial training, they come with varying degrees of experience. With the exception of the special missions units, many of the soldiers, sailors, and marines who become

SOF warriors may come directly from their initial basic/advanced/ infantry service training. Others may have two to eight years of service with conventional-branch units. All receive some type of formal physical, professional, and moral training during their SOF-specific training. In some cases this training is extensive. Marines new to the Marine Special Operations Command and soldiers fresh to the 75th Ranger Regiment will receive indoctrination and certification appropriate to those commands, but these initial training requirements are counted in months. Navy SEAL and Army Special Forces training is of the more-extensive variety. For the sake of brevity in this work and because my own experience (I've written books on both) encourages this approach, we will take a quick look at only SEAL and Army Special Forces training.

It takes a year or more to make a Navy SEAL out of a Navy sailor, although a SEAL is technically still a sailor. Some 80 percent of the new enlisted men come directly from Navy basic training, while the others derive from the fleet or the Marine Corps. The officers are primarily newly commissioned officers, with a sprinkling of officers who have had a single shipboard tour of duty. This is a year of famously challenging physical and professional training with dramatic rates of attrition. Candidly, it is part training and part testing. Half of this year is spent in basic SEAL training and half in an advanced-skill course called SEAL Qualification Training. Most of the value-based training takes place during basic SEAL training, which is called Basic Underwater Demolition/SEAL, or BUD/S, training. Here, again, there is much value in the informal, ad hoc training in ethics and warriorship that takes place during the physical and professional venues. And there is the highly influential presence of the SEAL instructors as role models. The SEALs have also adapted a mentoring program that supports the Navy's Core Values of Honor, Courage, Commitment, and also provides assistance to those in training who have special issues ranging from improper conduct to physical injury. The values training amounts to about sixteen hours of instruction that include formal classroom time, group discussion, and case study. Officers receive additional training that relates to leadership, ethics, and right conduct on the battlefield through specific training on the rules of engagements, human rights, and the Laws of Armed Conflict. SEAL officers, like their Special Forces officer counterparts, conduct much of their special operations training with their enlisted men.

Following this difficult year of SEAL training, the graduate SEALs (the survivors) will be assigned to a SEAL platoon at an active SEAL team. Depending on operational requirements and deployment rotations, new platoon SEALs may have as much as eighteen months of individual, platoon, and predeployment training before they step into the battlespace. Most of our new SEALs' training, as well as the predeployment preparation for the veterans, is built around a direct-action operational model. Navy SEALs have functioned well in the insurgent battlespace, but their training focuses on reconnaissance and direct-action mission profiles. I can say without qualification that few American warriors go in harm's way with more lengthy training or more time on their guns than our Navy SEALs.

Army Special Forces is another highly trained SOF component. It takes a year or more to make a Green Beret, and the rates of attrition in the Special Forces are as high as those for Navy SEALs. The new Special Forces recruits are a mix of experienced soldiers and new men who have come from OSUT with a three-week detour for Army airborne training. Unique to Army Special Forces is the seasoning of its officers. Officers reporting for Special Forces Training are veterans with four to six years of service in the conventional Army. Special Forces training, like SEAL training, has formal sessions that revisit and reinforce service core values. Also like the SEALs, the training cadres are held up to the new men both professionally and morally as role models. The Special Forces specifically screen its training-cadre officers in order to get the best back into the training pipeline. So what are the differences between Special Forces and the SEALs from the standpoint of the ethics and character-driven components of their training? First of all, Special Forces officers are segregated for some three months of their course for what amounts to graduate-level training in unconventional warfare and counterinsurgency. Following their basic SEAL training, SEAL officers attend the Junior Officers Training Course, which teaches, among other subjects, leadership and ethics.

Counterinsurgency warfare is the responsibility of the U.S. Army in general, but it is a priority with the Special Forces. Special Forces training, more than any training in any other branch of the military, is scenario based with an extensive infrastructure of role-players and interactive, simulated cross-cultural training venues. Language training is also mandatory for all Special Forces soldiers. Counterinsurgency training and cross-cultural training are perhaps not ethics or value training per se, but this kind of scenario-based instruction and interactive role-playing leads to a consideration and an awareness of right and wrong action on the battlefield and methods for dealing effectively with the locals in the insurgent battlespace. This scenario-based training puts a premium on understanding and respecting local customs and values, while at the same time taking no action that would compromise our own values. Army Special Forces may not have more allotted time under the heading of "values training" in their curricula than other SOF components, but I have found that the Green Berets are more disposed, from a training perspective, to do the right thing on the insurgent battlefield than any of our deployed ground-combat units. It's been my observation that SEAL training is highly tactical- and weapons-centric, while Army Special Forces training is more people- and cultural-centric. Few of our special operations warriors get more trigger time in training than our Navy SEALs; few of our special operators get more cross-cultural, human-terrain awareness training than our Green Berets.

The service-specific initial training venues—the boot camps—and the initial SOF training courses have several things in common. Both are periods of great change for the man in the arena—the kind of change that can redirect the course of a young life. In both, the training cadres have great influence over their students, whether they are warrior recruits or apprentice SOF warriors. These cadres represent what these young men want to become, and the sway they have over those who want to call themselves soldiers, marines, infantrymen, or special operators is incalculable. And finally, over the course of the training continuum, these training commands have near total control of the student population in the training pipelines. They own them. A great deal can be accomplished when you set the agenda of your students on a true 24/7 basis—and when your students are motivated to give you 110 percent.

Another factor that should not be overlooked is that these are all-male training scenarios. These training regimes are true rites of passage for young men, and there are not a lot of those left in America. I'll not go into whether this is a positive or a negative in the scheme of things for our nation, but if you're in the business of making ground-combat warriors, it's a good thing. This is not to say that there can be some dysfunctional macho issues to resolve or negative boy's-club cultural issues that have to be dealt with, but on balance it's a big help. The training cadres of these ground-combat training components are the gatekeepers. They control who will and will not join their ranks. So when they insist on a professional or physical standard, the young recruits or trainees will do all in their power to attain that standard. It's the same thing when a level of compliance is demanded for a moral standard. The service components and those who are charged with the responsibility for these basic and advanced schools have a duty to admit only those new warriors who have met rigorous professional, physical, *and* moral standards. I maintain that we do a terrific job with the professional and physical; the moral, to the point of this book, needs improvement.

Qualifying as a soldier, marine, SEAL, Green Beret, or Ranger is a milestone, and these rites of passage can be seminal events for young men. For some it is just a single step in life and may serve as an important basis for future personal growth. For others it may be the pinnacle of their achievements in life. In the case of the new Army infantryman, new Marine infantryman, or even the new special operator, he has made the transition from citizen to warrior, has separated himself from his former civilian life and civilian environment. His military mentors have done all in their power to reinforce the "good" civilian values that may have been his up to this point in time, and they have done all in their power to inculcate "good" military values. Just as significantly, and excepting for his drill instructors and military training cadre, our new soldier, marine, or special operator has had little contact with the culture he is about to enter. To take the newly minted warrior analogy a step further and permitting a generalization, his moral compass is as properly aligned as it is likely to get. Ahead of him are the challenges of active duty in a combat theater and the peer influences of his fellow soldiers and marines. Life in the training commands is *not* life in the operational units.

Within the special operations training pipelines, it is much the same. Those in SOF training may be fresh from OSUT or Navy boot camp, or they may have been in uniform for some time. Still, they are in a crucible of sorts, and their goal is to elevate their status to that of an elite warrior. If they succeed in training, they still face the cultural shift that comes with being a member of that elite special operations team. For all these new warriors—soldiers, marines, and special operators— leaving the training command is leaving the womb. Setting aside the issue of experience, which is not to be underestimated, the new men are physically and professionally prepared to join the operational units. Their biggest hurdle will be to integrate their personal value standard and the value set they received in training with the ethos of their new operational culture. It's an issue that goes to the heart of this work.

As a student of military training, I find the process of preparing new warriors to be one of the more fascinating and compelling change makers in American life. By that I mean it can create dramatic individual change and reorientation in a young life in a relatively short period of time. It can rival the change brought about by religious conversion and marriage—combined. By and large, this is a positive. Certainly in the areas of character and moral conduct, these military training forums are agents of change for the better. So if we train well and emphasize good values along with the professional and military skill sets, then why are we as a nation and a military still experiencing wrong conduct on the battlefield? My contention is that our problems are not with our military training; the issues lie within the culture of the operational units. No matter how rigorous the military training, the reorientation of values to a sustainable standard—one that will weather the culture of the operational units—is not easy. Our military training commands fight a war on two fronts. They must counter the negative values the new men bring with them from their civilian life. They must also fortify the new men with a set of military values that *may* be challenged by the entrenched culture of their new squad or platoon. Moreover, individual values—whether religious, parental, societal, or force-fed in military training—are severely challenged by modern military combat operations. The operational culture—the *real* culture of the military—is the issue here. In most cases it is good. Occasionally, contrary to command intent and usually in the absence of good leadership, it can allow for the dysfunctional. Ultimately this culture has a tremendous effect on right and wrong conduct, in combat and in garrison. In that same vein, we should never underestimate the pack factor.

Most of our young warriors have a compelling need to belong. This does not imply that they do not want to do the right thing. They simply want to be members of the club—the pack. It's what SEALs, marines, and street gangs have in common. That's why many enter the military; they want to belong to something greater than themselves as individuals, and they are willing to do just about anything to attain this goal. That's why when they reach that goal, duty in an operational unit, they will conform to the norms of that unit—that pack. And if that calls for setting aside a value set they learned or pledged themselves to in their earlier military training, many will do just that. So there are competing forces here. There is the issue of character that our young warrior learned within the confines of his military training. There is this need to belong and conform. And there are the decades of social imprinting that comes from growing up in America. Military training works very hard to neutralize negative societal values and to co-opt and reinforce those that are good, but it can only do so much. Contemporary American culture is a powerful influence. Every soldier and special operator brings something of this with him when he enters training. Let's take a closer look at these influences.

CHAPTER FOUR

Composition of the Force

As we've seen in the previous chapter, no small amount of attention and effort goes into training that relates to battlefield ethos and warrior honor. Most of this training is "front-loaded" and most heavily applied to new recruits and enlistees. For all but a few, this training will have been ongoing and integrated at all levels of their basic and advanced training. By the time they reach the operational units, all of our soldiers, marines, and special operators have sat through classes and participated in discussions on ethics, character, and values. In a few cases these subjects have been addressed in scenario- and situational-based training, although rarely are they developed to the level as practiced in Army Special Forces training. As for conventional-force values training, credit the Marine Corps for its efforts to make values and ethos instruction an interactive process in small discussion groups and to acknowledge preservice values as they relate to what is expected in compliance with its service core values. In reality, all the services do this. As for the operational units, moral issues and issues of right and wrong are addressed as part of most predeployment ROE indoctrination, in least insofar as they relate to the rules of engagement. So, at this juncture, you might therefore be tempted to ask: If there is such an emphasis on good warriorship in the training commands, and the troops are getting at least some moral conditioning before deployment, why is it that some of our units and individual warriors are still doing wrong things on the battlefield? I'm of the opinion that the information is not being made relevant to those who have to fight on an insurgent battlefield, and that when it is, this information is often negated and made irrelevant by the contemporary small-unit military culture. I'm not the only one who sees it this way.

In the fall of 2007, a "survey" was taken of our forces in Iraq in an attempt to learn just how many of our soldiers and marines might be operating outside accepted standards of battlefield conduct. I've been unable to get the details of this study, but I'm betting it surfaced some very revealing and even sensitive information. The survey results prompted General Petraeus to issue his May 2007 letter to all uniformed personnel in the multinational force in Iraq. The general was ambiguous about the survey, but not about the need for change. In his letter (again, see Appendix I) he addressed the issue in a straightforward manner that has been all too often lacking in theater-command leadership regarding battlefield conduct. The general acknowledged that wrong action has and is taking place, and that it is not only illegal, but also counterproductive to the mission. Few senior commanders will publicly acknowledge that their troops, albeit a minority, are acting inappropriately and move to take this kind of action. At the time of its publication, any number of journalists took this as an indictment of the Bush-Cheney-Rumsfeld policy in Iraq and an admission of an official policy of torture and mistreatment of detainees. I read it as an indication that we have culture issues at the squad and platoon level that has led to wrong battlefield conduct. And I can only imagine that when this letter came down the chain of command, it left more than a few brigade and battalion commanders asking, "Is he talking about *my* troops?"

So, where are we going with this? I believe that when our warriors conduct themselves in a manner that is outside the moral envelope of right conduct, this is not how they were trained, and, collectively, they know it is wrong. Such behavior is not the intent of the senior military leadership, and it's under the radar of our senior battlespace commanders. Furthermore, it is in violation of the rules of engagement, and very damaging to the mission. It's a breakdown—a disconnect between command policy and what is taking place on the ground.

How does this happen, and why does this happen? Is it a lapse in conduct or something more systemic? And what can be done about it? The what-can-be-done question we'll address in later sections of this work. For now, and because this is a moral as well as a military issue, let's start at the beginning and look at the raw material—the new recruits that are the lifeblood of our armed forces. On average, our military must recruit 10 percent of its force each year to maintain current manpower levels. Who are these new recruits, and where do they come from? We have addressed the culture of the warrior, historically and in the context of what is needed to field a modern ground force. Now let's take a look at those currently entering the military and the culture that formed them.

As a general grouping, the young men who are candidates for our ground-force components are the Millennials—those born between roughly 1980 and 2000. They've also been labeled as Generation Y or Echo Boomers. There are plenty of them in uniform, and more are coming. As with all generational classes, they are special and distinctive, with their own positive and negative characteristics as those relate to military service. Applying generalizations to individual conduct is always a dangerous business, but Millennials seem, when compared to other generations, to be more ambitious, more brand conscious, more mobile in that they move more often, and have more experience with family breakdown and divorce. They seem to be more highly influenced by their peers and their workplace culture. This generation is more open-minded about sexual and romantic encounters and personal attachments, and they are more tolerant of alternative lifestyles. They are exponentially more tech savvy than any previous generation. Their loyalties can be fierce and shifting. A great deal has been written about the Millennials—by employers, journalists, sociologists, and philosophers.

They've been variously described as hardworking, impatient, clever, resourceful, lazy, team-orientated, and incorrigible. They are said to be self-centered and narcissist—the "me" generation. So it's the military's task, as with any employer, to find a way to harness the Millennials' potential as well as to effectively deal with any baggage that may accompany them into the workplace. Demanding that they be different or insisting that they summarily disregard the factors that shaped them is simply not an option. The extent to which the military can deal with the Millennials' array of characteristics and potentially conflicting values will have a great bearing in the success of that generation's soldiers, sailors, airmen, and marines, and how they function in our ground-combat units.

Each generation has its own perspectives and myopia in the way it views its world, its America. It is an incremental, evolutionary part of our society. In a very true sense, it is America. Those currently in the armed forces, and certainly those just coming into the military, while perhaps distinctive, are often said to be a reflection of our society at large. I take the position that this mirroring of society is only partly true. This may have been more the case when our nation had a draft and when the net cast for those who were made to serve in uniform yielded a more representative sampling. Yet, even then, I'm not so sure how much those draft-era recruits who engaged in ground-combat operations mirrored the general population. Then, as now, we're looking at only a segment of the population and a segment of the military. We had a draft when we fought the war in Vietnam, but an overwhelming number of those engaged in active combat then were volunteers. Those of draft age who wanted not to become engaged in that ground war could enlist in the Navy or the Air Force. Many did. So at least some of this ground-force dynamic—then, as now—is the same. This was certainly the case for those going back on their second and third deployments. In Vietnam, if you were drafted and sent into ground combat with a line unit in the Army, you only had to do a single one-year tour and you were done. Those who served multiple tours in *that* war were clearly volunteers. The demands and requirements of our military change with time, but what we ask of those who fight on the ground has not changed all that much. I think it's safe to say that changes in our society over the last half a century have occurred at a far more rapid pace than any changes within our military.

The key demographic for the military in the business of war-fighting on the ground is the combat-age male, so some of what may have been skewed regarding societal norms when we had a draft is still true today. Even as we look at the tens of thousands deployed to Iraq and Afghanistan today, only a small fraction of those are in units engaged in active ground combat or conducting armed counterinsurgency activities. Said another way, we're look-ing at the personnel on the ground whose duties and responsibili-ties are governed by the laws of war and the rules of engagement. This does not mean that someone *has* to be in a ground combat unit to do the wrong thing—witness what took place at Abu Ghraib, where a military police unit was responsible for the wrongdoing—but our focus here is conduct in a tactical environment.

Our military has need for a broad range of skills and disciplines, and has in place a comprehensive infrastructure for training person-nel to meet these diverse requirements. Those skills that relate to ground-combat operations are a subset of general military skills, although in the areas of character, discipline, and ethics, all recruits initially receive much of the same training. For our purposes, the male recruits coming into our military have traditionally been in the eighteen- to twenty-four-year-old range, but today that range is probably closer to eighteen to twenty-eight. This might seem like a large pool, with some 20 million males in that range and close to 2 million young men turning eighteen every year. But as stated earlier, this is a very diverse and dynamic group, and there are both com-peting and limiting factors at work on this targeted demographic. A good many of these young men are looking to attend college or will be seeking vocational or civilian training following high school. Many others are bound to their communities by familial or social ties. More than a few simply don't want to serve in the military. Rightly or wrongly, they perceive the military as repressive, restrictive, and even immoral. Many are turned away by peer pressure, and more than a few take the view that the military is the employer of last resort. There are conscientious and religious reasons for not considering military service. A fair number of these young men simply fear the acknowledged loss of freedom that accompanies the often painful transition from citizen to soldier. And a great many young men simply don't think of the military as an option; those who do may reject it for some irrational or very real reason. In spite of the recruiting ads on TV, the boot-camp experience and the life of a private soldier or marine are not treated well by the TV networks or by Hollywood. So, there are a great number of potential young males who might make good candidates for the military and who could well benefit from what the military has to offer, but they choose to make themselves unavailable.

Then there is the issue of individual suitability. To field a ground-combat force, the military is looking for reasonably smart, reasonably fit young men who are attentive and motivated to work and learn. They may not have to be our brightest and best, but there are mental and physical minimums to the business of soldiering. Those who qualify are also in demand by corporations and businesses in the manufacturing and service sectors. What makes for a good hire at Starbucks, Boeing, or UPS also makes for a good recruit in the military. The intellectual, physical, and emotional shortcomings that would cause these companies to turn a young man down—and they turn down a great many—might well make that same person unsuitable for military service. Some branches of the military have recently eased their physical, intelligence, and age restrictions. Yet in speaking with recruiters, I'm surprised at just how many high school seniors simply can't qualify to get into the military. Those who can are the ones who have options, and they could as easily chose a good job with FedEx or the local fire department.

Perhaps the most honest and realistic measure of the "good" in our society as applied to desirable virtues in this demographic is the metric of those who hire at the entry-level position. Both the military and the private sector are looking for the same positive traits:

intelligence, honesty, diligence, loyalty, and so on. They also want to eliminate people with negative attributes—the criminals, the dysfunctional, those with learning or social disabilities, and the uneducated. Both the military and the private sector are best served if they can screen candidates for the characteristics they want and deselect those with unfavorable traits. Additionally, the military will have more stringent physical requirements than their civilian competitors. Yet for both the military and the civilian sector, the key metric is intelligence. Simply stated, the best clerks, waiters, policemen, health-care workers, barbers, bank tellers, and soldiers are the smart ones. Smart people are always in demand.

Candidates for military service undergo a number of tests. Among these, the military has some very comprehensive aptitude, or vocational, exams. Chief among them is the Armed Services Vocational Aptitude Battery (ASVAB). In reality, it's an IQ test. There are other indicators of suitability for military service besides aptitude, but what this testing process really determines, and what the military wants to know, is just how smart a guy is. Motivation, physical capability, and even some aspects of what constitutes good character can be addressed through training and conditioning, but intelligence and, to a great extent, mental discipline cannot be taught.

The military, as we know, has a unique and important advantage over its civilian competition—it has boot camp. Business and industry have their training and indoctrination programs, but in no way are they able to exercise the total control of their new hires like the military is able to do in basic training. Much can be accomplished during this period of near total control in the way of teaching, conditioning, and evaluation. Yet it does not change intelligence. The other thing it cannot do is erase or fully overwrite some two decades of the social imprinting that comes from growing up in America.

It comes down to this: The chief objective of all military training, basic and advanced, is to equip the soldier with the physical, professional, and moral tools to serve. This is certainly the case for those engaged in ground combat—those who fight in battle. Professionally, this means mastering the weaponry, technology, and tactics of modern warfare, whether that is maneuver warfare or insurgent warfare. The military is far more sophisticated today than it was a generation ago—even more than just before the attacks of 9/11. So are the men and women coming of military age. The smarter and more motivated the soldier, the easier the task of mastering the current military skill sets. Physically, time and attention are paid to helping the recruit become fit and stay fit, as well as choosing the right methodology and venues for physical training. There's more to it than push-ups, running, and military drill. The physical programs currently used by the military are designed to promote strength and stamina on the battlefield as well as to prevent injury. This physical regime includes a proper diet, which in many cases can be a dramatic change for the better for those coming into the military. Americans today are probably less fit and consume more fast food than they did a generation ago, but this is relatively easy to fix among recruits. In short, both professional and physical training are well formatted and refined, and changes and advances in both these areas are relatively easy to merge into existing doctrine and training. Perhaps the most challenging is the moral side of this three-part equation. Arguably it's the most important, and it's certainly the most difficult to make an integrated part of the squad and platoon culture. As discussed in the previous chapter, character and warrior ethos training are front-loaded during the early postinduction training period. Past these highly formatted initial training curricula, attention to the physical and the professional is ongoing, but that which is allotted to the ethical and moral conduct of war can vary greatly. What happens in the operational units and, to the point, what should happen in both operational and predeployment training will be addressed later.

There is an additional factor that needs to be mentioned here—one separate and distinct from the professional, physical, and moral aspects of warrior development. It relates to service recruitment and how America fights extended wars with our modern all-volunteer force. After 9/11, this nation went to war, but we didn't really mobilize for war. Because we were attacked here in our homeland, the service components enjoyed a surge of volunteers. Then we simply took our standing force, along with these new soldiers and marines, and began to deploy them to meet new operational requirements. Our reserve components were also mobilized as needed to augment shortfalls in the active force. Those in uniform, active and reserve, had to adjust to a wartime deployment rotation, something that was unknown to most of these volunteers. With the exception of a few selected special operations units, being in uniform had heretofore been a preparing-for-war business, not a going-to-war business. The events of 9/11 changed all that. After the initial successes in Afghanistan and Iraq, the prolonged nature of this conflict settled in. Our commander in chief spoke to a long struggle, but for those in uniform, that long struggle takes on a different meaning after the second or third combat rotation. For those of us here at home, it takes a different meaning with the repatriation of our combat dead and wounded.

Many military professionals welcomed the challenge of combat duty, at least initially. This is not to say they love war, but it was a chance to put those years of training into practice. Our nation was attacked, and the call to arms was righteous. Others found that multiple tours in harm's way were simply not what they wanted. Reservists were recalled to active duty—and kept on active duty. Those on active duty found their deployments lengthened and their home rotations cut short. Many were not allowed to leave active/reserve service at the end of their enlistment; they were kept in uniform due to the stop-loss provision—a procedure that allows for the wartime extension of enlistment contracts. Now, with the drawdown in Iraq and more attention given to Afghanistan, the services are still looking to fill their enlistment quotas. It's not an easy sell, even when economic times are difficult. The post-9/11 patriotic volunteers have finished their initial enlistment, and those held involuntarily in uniform will have been released. Those who were "caught" in the peacetime military prior to 9/11 and found it not to their liking will also have left the service. For potential volunteers, certainly those who want to join our ground-force components, we are still a nation at war. Those new soldiers and marines in the infantry units and the special operations components know they will deploy again and again into harm's way. The new recruits for the all-volunteer force, and those who enlist to serve in ground-force units, know they are volunteering for combat. For many considering military service, this changes the appeal of serving in uniform.

There is a parallel issue that accompanies the recruitment and training of new warriors that bears directly on the moral posture of our deployed military. This is not an insignificant topic, and it has helped to shape the specific demographic of ground-force-suitable candidates. Every generation, including my own during its time, brings an assortment of biases, baggage, and predispositions with it into military service. I'm certainly no sociologist, but in addition to those Millennial attributes listed earlier, the current generation of young men have been subjected to and conditioned in an environment that has much more media-generated violence than previous generations. First, there is the influence of on-screen violence on television and in the movies. Of these the most influential and pervasive is TV. On average, children in America watch three to four hours of television daily. In many families kids spend more time with the TV than with their parents or other children, or even in school. It's a powerful influence, and an increasingly violent one.

Experts and psychologists in the field agree that a diet of TV violence tends to make adolescents immune or indifferent to violence. In addition, they often imitate what they watch, and see violence as a behaviorial model or a way to solve problems. Even in homes where there is no sibling or parental violence, kids who watch a lot of TV seem to be more aggressive and physical in their interaction with others. Aggressiveness and confrontational behavior have their place in military ground combat, but in this context it must be restrained, focused, and disciplined. TV violence, when imitated by adolescents, is seldom reasoned or restrained. It's simply learned behavior.

Along with my nonsociologist credentials, I'll acknowledge my limited understanding of anthropology, but it seems to me something fundamental is taking place here. Going back in time, children learned behavior from their family, clan, and community/tribal entities. Trade and artisan skills were apprenticed and passed on to the next generation. I think it's much the same with violence and aggression. In past aggressive cultures such as the Mongol, the Spartan, and the Viking, and even in some Indian tribes, young aspiring warriors listened to the tales of conquest and warrior-ship around campfires. They saw the results of a successful raid in terms of spoils of war and honor afforded the warrior. Violence and aggression were rewarded and admired, much as we now value and reward a good education or a good work ethic. Yet today we seldom sit around campfires, and far too few families sit around the dining-room table. We're busy. The rearing of our children is still done in the home, but often in a very competitive and bustling environment. There also seems to be a shrinking influence of the adult commu-nity at large. A few small towns and close neighborhoods still exist in which a citizen on the street will discipline someone else's child for inappropriate behavior, but this is becoming rare. Our schools are places in which discipline often means the absence of physical violence in the classroom. It's my sense that disruptive behavior in general, if not violence, often rides just below the surface; it is held in check more than it is actively discouraged. All of these factors allow Hollywood-style violence on TV and in film to be a growing influence on our nation's youth.

This may seem like a harsh indictment of the entertainment industry, but unrestrained, on-screen violence is a fact of our mod-ern life. Every year it seems to become more graphic and aggres-sive, and more accepted as suitable entertainment. Yet its effects are hard to measure. I'd like to believe that kids take the violence and aggressive behavior they see only as cartoon violence, much like Road Runner tricking Wile E. Coyote into a fall from a steep cliff—that they don't mistake this for reality. And I'd also like to believe that any imitative behavior that may result from a diet of TV violence is simply an adolescent phase—that kids will grow out of it and move on to more rational and sociable conduct. Yet I'm not so sure that the seeds of dysfunction are not being sown. There are still good messages amid the undercurrent of growing on-screen violence; wrongdoers get sent to jail, and those who enforce the law still prevail. The police and the firemen and the justice system still win more than they lose. But I also perceive a subtle message that there is virtue in wrong behavior. I find it in the swagger of the felons, and the glitter and lifestyle of drug dealers and corporate cheats. It says that respect and merit are afforded those who operate outside the law—that there is some nobility in being tough and bad, even brutal. This message often carries a tolerance for, and even a certain celebration of, violence.

Yet not all is bad in America. The moderating influences of good parenting, good teachers, good peer values, religion, and positive role models count for a great deal. Most of us have known young people who have gone through an antisocial, rebellious stage and emerged whole and cordial, and moved on in a positive direction. Quite often the realities of intimate relationships, workaday life, and increasing responsibility become effective antidotes for the violent diversion that often passes for entertainment. Perhaps the violence on TV is just escapism for those of us who lead bland lives. But sometimes it isn't. For some children, film and TV violence mirror what goes on in their communities and neighborhoods. The nightly news only reinforces the fact that reality is not pacific—that aggression and hostility are effective tools in the world. Others may seem unaffected by on-screen violence, but those hours and years in front of the TV have residual influence; there is an imprinting of the dysfunctional that may only emerge during times of stress or in certain environments conducive to violence. Some of those souls, perhaps even a disproportionate number of them, enter military service.

Several disturbing themes emerging on television and in popular culture are worth mentioning here. Among these are the reality shows. "Questionable-reality" is probably a better term for these staged competitions. They are rife with posturing, in-your-face confrontations and win-at-all-cost messages. In these programs real people are put in unreal situations while dysfunctional and duplicitous conduct becomes the focus of the competition. All this is tightly edited and packaged to appeal to what I can only assume are viewers who see this as real. The only reality is that the participants are clearly not professional actors, but they are aggressive and they are confrontational. I've personally known a few of these reality-show players. Off screen and in real life, they are perfectly normal, even exemplary in their accomplishments, but it's as if they're seduced by their role in these competitive TV dramas. Yet it's their on-screen personae that are known and remembered, not the positive contributions they may have made. To be honest, I don't quite understand the fascination with which many follow these programs.

Another kind of reality show that provides more of a selective variety are the true-crime shows, which feature car chases, car crashes, contested arrests, and the like. These are often on the A&E network. These often feature low-resolution, amateur video from a handheld camera in a helicopter or footage from a police cruiser. If there is a vehicle crash or a confrontation between police and a fugitive, that clip is played over and over at increasing magnification. Similar to these are the documentaries of unsolved crimes, usually macabre events that try to re-create a particularly heinous murder or torturing. These shows feature interviews with investigators, county sheriffs, and prosecutors, all locals who recall the event and are ready to speak about the tragedy and the violence of the act. There is much speculation as to how and why the crime took place. If the crime is unresolved, there is speculation about who may have done it; if the perpetrators are known, we get to learn about them.

Another celebration of violence is professional wrestling. I'm not sure who are the more dysfunctional—the guys in the ring or those at ringside. This is chilling stuff. I'm not aware of any spectacle like it. While these shows feature well-choreographed and well-rehearsed performances, events sponsored by World Wrestling Entertainment generate a great deal of staged rage. These shows may be silly and bizarre, and the participants near caricatures of athletes, but they are violent, and they do promote and showcase physical aggression. Professional wrestling is a pretend blood sport—often with obscene gestures and sexual innuendo. Even so, somewhere close to 10 million people watch this stuff on TV. The ratings for these shows are quite high. Imagine! It would be easy to chalk this off to people with too much time on their hands or those with daytime jobs so boring that this passes for stimulation or amusement. But the disturbing fact is that 15 percent of the viewers are under the age of twelve. Well over a million grade-schoolers watch this programming, and probably as many more in their teens. Not all of these kids see these steroid-charged actors as cartoon characters, and probably more than I would care to guess try the hold-of-the-week, or the gouge-of-the-week, on their little brother. Professional wrestling is probably a favorite program of neighborhood bullies.

One of the recent developments in media-driven sports violence is the emerging popularity of mixed martial arts (MMA) and ultimate-fighting contests—the latter in the form of the UFC (Ultimate Fighting Championship). This is a truly interesting phenomenon. Such contests became commercial in the early nineties when promoters sought to interest audiences in a contest to decide just which sport/discipline/fighting style was the best—boxing, wrestling, karate, jujitsu, and the like. More simply, can a wrestler beat a boxer? These no-holds-barred events quickly attracted a loyal home video and pay-per-view following, along with some unfavorable press coverage. More than half the states banned the contests, and politicians such as Senator John McCain, who called it "human cockfighting," became vocal critics. A succession of promoters managed to tame these new and popular fighting contests and bring them within bounds of acceptable media promotion. What evolved throughout the decade were events that came to use a mix of all these fighting styles and were promoted as no-rules, ultimate-fighting contests. A sport, for which a claim of legitimacy can be made, emerged that did in fact incorporate multiple fighting disciplines. Currently the sport features an octagon-shaped "cage" in place of a ring that makes the contest spectator friendly. There also evolved a set of rules that allowed for state-sanctioned events. In 2004 and 2005 UFC/MMA contests essentially went mainstream and never looked back. In 2006 these contests surged past boxing and the professional wrestling in pay-per-view revenues. Following the highly successful *Survivor* format, *The Ultimate Fighter* was launched on Spike TV, and its popularity continues to be meteoric. Anheuser-Busch and Harley-Davidson now sponsor what has become the Ultimate Fighting Championship. Top-tier UFC fighters are now sports and media celebrities who may soon rival football and basketball stars. Certainly among those who follow the UFC, they are sports icons.

So what do the UFC contests have to do with the military and those entering the military? This form of fighting is most popular within the demographic that is the target of the military recruiters. Additionally, *some* of the skill sets and conditioning routines of the UFC fighters have *some* applicability to those skills that are useful in ground-combat operations. We'll deal with UFC's effect on recruiting first. Those charged with finding the right young men for the military, specifically those suited to becoming ground combatants, see eighteen- to twenty-six-year-old UFC fans as excellent prospects. To this end the military, specifically the U.S. Army, has entered into a relationship with the UFC that will allow UFC/MMA-type events to be held at military facilities and create MMA-type club activities on base. I found it interesting that when I went to the UFC Web site, I found a link to the GoArmy.com Web site. I also saw commercial links to Harley-Davidson motorcycles, Bud Light, energy supplements, singles online dating, ultimate-fighter action photos and videos (with lots of posturing), a UFC gallery of scantily clad females, and online UFC shopping that ranges from the athletic to the very strange. The mechanics of the Web site are as good as those for Dell or Toyota. Neither Dell nor Toyota has links to the U.S. Army.

Second, as previously mentioned, the skills of ultimate fighting do have some physical bearing on those needed for ground combat. Actually, it's not so much the skills of punching, striking, or grappling that transfer as it is the conditioning. While I find that the hype and fanfare that surround the UFC and MMA is a bit much, there is no doubt in my mind that those who fight at the upper levels in these competitions are superb athletes. Their training and conditioning routines are most impressive. Anyone who trains anywhere near the level of these martial arts or mixed martial arts fighters will usually exceed the physical requirements for military duty. Past this physical conditioning, I'm not sure how much skill-based transference there is. As we will see in the later sections of this work, the *only* true ultimate fighting, save for street-gang or criminal-related activity, is military combat. In ground combat, winners live and losers die. When the fight is a fight to the death, sport- and ring-based rules are often counterproductive.

Perhaps the most detrimental message or negative imprint that comes from all of these media-delivered fighting events, reality shows, staged dramas, or what have you is the posturing. This self-centered, macho, in-your-face attitude is a direct opposite of the qualities of duty, honor, courage, commitment, excellence, self-restraint, and humility—the very characteristics that are at the core of a warrior. What I would call the negative influences of American culture seem to fall heaviest on those very Americans who are needed by our military to fulfill ground-combat roles. So a great deal of what military training is about is to reverse and override those counterproductive tendencies that are the antitheses of right warrior conduct. This deprogramming, if you will, is a daunting challenge. It asks a boot-camp drill sergeant to undo in a few months what might have been two decades of inappropriate behavior modeling. And it doesn't end with boot camp; media influence in our society is a part of both our popular and our military cultures. Our off-duty soldiers and marines are fed a steady diet of media programming, even on deployment. I've been to some remote forward operating bases in Iraq, and there always seems to be a dish antenna and a wall-mounted flat-screen monitor. When our soldiers, marines, and special operators are not in training or on patrol, they watch TV. It's as if there is simply no getting away from this influence.

It seems as if I've painted quite a dark picture of our culture and the effects that culture has on America's youth—specifically those entering military service and those on active service. But as previously mentioned, not all is bad in America. Amid all of that which seems overly commercial and dysfunctional and mindlessly violent, much of what the military teaches and stands for is appealing. The value set that serves American warriors present is much like those of American warriors past. While there have been changes in the methods of war and the attitudes toward war, the virtues of the warrior have changed little. As media and commercial forces evolve and vie for our attention, their message doesn't always resonate. There are many young Americans who are looking for some anchor or fixed reference of personal values and personal worth. So the military can be an attractive option for those who may not buy into the commercialism or the violence. This is often seen in the recruiting advertisements—the ones that may often precede a sporting event or a UFC competition. These often promote job training and adventure, but they also focus on honor, duty, and service.

The generation we have labeled as the Millennials are coming of age amid a great deal of uncertainty, social change, and mixed messages. As previously mentioned, they bring with them a great deal of talent and potential. They join a standing force that may be the best our nation has ever put into the field. Yet it remains for the military to recruit the new men, mold them, and channel their talent and potential into virtuous warrior conduct, from the basic-training venues into the operational units and then onto the battlefield. Yet the Millennials bring a great deal of baggage with them—that is to say, the social and cultural values that are *not* helpful to good warriorship. In this chapter I've gone into some of the aspects of American society that have to be reversed or brought into line with what is expected of those who conduct ground-combat operations. I did this for good reason, as those same negative social and cultural issues are waiting for our newly minted soldiers, marines, and special operators when they finish basic training. Our warriors coming out of the military basic/initial training programs are like those being released from drug-rehab programs. They're clean, and many have a new and fresh outlook on life, one that's in keeping with their new status as American warriors. But there are forces out there that will challenge their new moral orientation—forces such as the media, the social scene, and even old friends.

In addition to the lingering effects of old values and old friends, there is the challenging influence of the operational units the new warriors will soon join. In the final chapters of this book, we will look at the impact of that critical period between basic training and the battlefield. If the moral health of the operational unit is good and small-unit leadership is good, then our new warrior will likely make the transition from right conduct in training to right conduct in garrison and to right conduct in combat. If they're not, then the road to the battlefield can be a moral minefield. It is my belief that there is no more critical time in the moral grounding of a young warrior than that period between the completion of basic/initial training and the eve of his first deployment.

CHAPTER FIVE

Toward an Effective Tactical Ethos

Several years ago I was speaking with the commanding officer of the Naval Special Warfare Center in Coronado, California. Among many responsibilities, he was charged with taking sailors and making them into Navy SEALs. When he arrived at the center, he felt, as I did, that more could to be done in the way of values, ethics, and character development for our young SEALs in training. He set out to do that very thing.

"I was pretty naive when I began this," he told me. "My goal was to send new SEALs to the operational teams who were uniformly stamped with a sense of honor and good moral values. This was to be a four-year tour, and I felt that if I could accomplish this over four years, I could have a lasting impact on our SEAL teams—that I could make a real difference." This seemed like a good and noble plan to me—to make SEALs who were professionally and physically trained to standard, but with more emphasis on character training and a deeper sense of a warrior ethic. Done over four years, it could have a dramatic impact on the moral health of the SEAL teams. "But I don't think our efforts here at the training command have made much of a difference," he continued. "Oh, we shined them up like new money all right and sent them off to the teams, but when they got to the operational platoons, they immediately adapted to the culture of their platoon. If that SEAL platoon had good leadership and practiced good values, the new guys took that on as what was expected of them. But if there were bad actors or pirates in the platoon, hard drinkers and bar fighters, and that kind of conduct was allowed or tolerated, then the new SEALs would immediately fall in with that kind behavior. No matter what we do in the training command, it's still all about the culture in the operational platoons."

I think this is a fair assessment of the issue and the problem, and one not just limited to Navy SEAL platoons. By that I mean that it's all about the culture that exists within our small-unit, ground-combat, operational components. More specifically, conduct is largely governed by the culture of that unit. This extends to right and wrong conduct on the part of individual warriors *and* what is tolerated by those who may themselves act properly. On first glance it might seem that character, virtue, and the expectation of right conduct, if effectively taught in the training commands, would have more of a lasting effect on the new warriors. Sometimes it does, but I suspect that this only happens when a soldier, marine, or special operator comes from a value-based background—one with strong family values, religious influence, or positive role models. Many of our new warriors do enter the service with a strong sense of values and fully understand what is right and wrong. For the morally grounded new men, the journey from a family/community ethos to a warrior ethos is not a difficult or dramatic transition. It is an extension of what they know to be right and good. For others, the notion of character or of conduct that is in keeping with a warrior ethic is very new. Traditional warrior values such as duty, honor, commitment, restraint, humility, and compassion have only been recently learned. For them, these are novel ideas and not in keeping with their peer values or all of those hours and years of watching television.

I fully agree with my friend at the SEAL training facility: the platoon culture is everything. By extension, this also applies to the squad-centric and even company-centric cultures. Our ground-combat components receive a continuous stream of young men who are seeking to belong. They are pack-orientated, team-orientated animals entering a very male and very hierarchical world. It's the world of the warrior culture. So it should be no surprise that the new men should favor conformity when they reach their operational components and want to blend in. As it applies to the issues of right and wrong, the training our new warriors receive may or may not stand up within the context of what is accepted practice in their operational unit. Navy SEAL training, the basic training along with the advanced Qualification Training, requires a full year—that's a full year on top of Navy boot camp. Compare this with the Army and the Marines, who complete their basic/advanced training in a third of that time. If the SEAL trainers cannot instill values that can buck the culture of the operational SEAL platoons, then who can? What can any of our basic-training venues do in the way of character and ethics formation that can stand up to the tightly bound warrior brotherhood of these small tactical units? In this chapter and the next, we'll explore what might be done to improve the moral health of this small-unit culture with the objective of reducing wrong conduct on the battlefield.

As previously stated, I believe that the notion of a warrior ethos and what constitutes good character are being addressed in basic military training reasonably well. The fundamentals that define the moral transition from citizen to soldier are in place; there is a clear understanding among those who have this training responsibility that this is both an important and a dynamic process. There are continuous refinements and adjustments as more is learned about the transformation that needs to take place in the making of a warrior. American culture, which rears our young warriors, is constantly changing. So is the role of American warriors on the modern battlefield. It then follows that the process that grooms our warriors must also change as better information and better methods make themselves available. So as it applies to modern ground-combat requirements, the training commands are doing a good job of balancing the physical, the professional, and the moral in molding American soldiers out of American civilians.

The curriculum in the training commands—or, in militaryspeak, the POIs (plans of instruction)—change and evolve slowly. Perhaps the biggest variable, and conceivably the most important one, are the training cadres. New recruits are quite impressionable, and most will remember their first drill instructor or drill sergeant in some detail. For most new recruits, he is their first military role model; they see in him what they want to be, and, in many ways, he *is* the military to them. So it is in the interest of the service components that we post our very best soldiers, marines, and special operators to the training commands. This has not always been the case. In the decade prior to 9/11, most of the good senior noncommissioned officers in our ground-combat units wanted to remain operational; training duty was not that attractive for them. Some of these veterans viewed service in the training commands as babysitting duty. Others simply relished the tactical challenges in a combat-ready unit. In the relative peacefulness of the nineties, especially following the First Gulf War, there was a feeling in the military that something was going to happen—somehow, somewhere there was going to be a conflict. Accompanying this feeling was a sense on the part of our veteran warriors that the last place they wanted to be when the fighting broke out was in the training command. Immediately following 9/11, virtually all of the good professionals wanted to be with their operational units. A set of orders to the training command kept a warrior on the sidelines, away from the action. Those "caught" in the training commands on 9/11 chafed to get back to their operational units and to the fight.

Today, it is my sense that we are in fact getting our best and most experienced veterans into the training commands and involved with the critical business of making new warriors. Part of this is due to command intent. Our senior commanders now understand that the success of their ground-combat components, especially in light of the demands of insurgency warfare, is closely linked with right conduct on the battlefield. This begins with the proper grooming of the new troops, so the best of our senior enlisted and junior officer leadership is being cycled back to the training commands. Even prior to and right after the attacks of 9/11, senior commanders and program managers were insisting that some of the more capable warriors assume the role of trainers, but it was a tough sell. Today, it's an easier sell. Part of this is due to the length of the war. Early on, most career veterans were intent on staying in combat rotation, even as that made for multiple combat tours. Now that we've been at this going on nine years, the combat-experienced are also the combat-weary, and many of them are now welcoming a few years out of deployment rotation. Never in the history of the all-volunteer force has there been this level of combat experience in our operational components, nor in our military training cadres.

Veterans being cycled back to the training commands are carefully screened for their professionalism and character, which only adds to the quality of the initial training curricula. This suggests that the services are doing a good job of preparing the new warriors—work that needs to continue *and* evolve to meet the changing nature of military recruits. This leaves us with an important dilemma: how do we close the gap between the good values being taught in basic/ initial training and the occasional absence of those values in the battlespace? This issue relates directly to the culture of the operational squads and platoons. It seems to be a systemic issue, but it's more complex than that. What makes for a good squad or platoon as opposed to a bad squad or platoon? Ten or twenty good or bad men? I believe that two or three influential individuals in a squad or platoon can wreak havoc with the unit culture and the mission. These few can create corrosive, pirate-type subcultures. They are not new; they've been a part of our military for some time. While these bad actors and their bad actions are never good, they are particularly harmful in an insurgency, in which restraint is central to the mission and respect for the local populations is critical.

In the latter stages of an insurgency, as we appear to be in Iraq, conditions exist that seem to invite wrong behavior. With the resurgence of the police and Iraqi security forces, there is very little real fighting to be done. Our troops are there to train the Iraqis and keep the peace. Yet it's still dangerous business. Keeping the peace means foot and vehicular patrols, and these invite an occasional insurgent attack—one in which there may be little opportunity for response or counterattack. When there is a call for an armed response, that required action may be highly restrictive and proportional. This restraint may be the only course of action that is in keeping with the mission, and this can be very frustrating. For those engaged in training the locals, that too can be frustrating, especially given that most of our professional warrior training is geared to offensive combat operations, not the training of others. And then there's the boredom and inactivity that accompany most deployments in an insurgent battlespace. I've had more than one lieutenant or first sergeant tell me that managing expectations about actual combat and dealing with boredom are among their chief concerns in Iraq. It seems as if many of the issues of bad conduct, at least in part, are sparked by isolated insurgent activity along with the frustration of training others to do what our military professionals themselves may have spent years training to do. And boredom in the battlespace often leads to wrong behavior.

Another issue that can spark bad conduct is revenge. Many of our veterans returning to the active theaters have had a friend or platoon mate killed or wounded. They often want to get back some of their own. Issues of revenge and payback are deeply rooted in our warrior culture, as well as in our media culture. It's hyped on TV and in the movies. We remember the battleship *Maine* and Pearl Harbor and 9/11. And it gets more personal when you can put a face to a brother who has fallen as a result of enemy action. Revenge, like boredom, can lead to acts that are neither discriminate nor proportional, and are very harmful to counterinsurgency operations.

For these reasons I believe the seeds of wrong conduct are embedded in the small-unit culture of our ground-combat components. In most cases these seeds are well managed and under control. Occasionally they are just below the surface, and vigilance is needed. Addressing these issues requires changes in that culture, or at least the mechanics to deal with them when they emerge. On first pass, this might seem like an easy fix to an isolated problem, but it's not. As previously mentioned, there are expectations about going into combat, and we need to manage those expectations. Even when there is only a small chance of active combat or sustained combat operations, a prudent military leader will prepare for it. The old military adage "hope for the best, prepare for the worst" applies. But when the requirements of the battlespace call for noncombat activity and restraint, there can be problems. Combat veterans can become cynics and question command intent; new soldiers see little prospect of becoming like those they most admire—the combat veterans. This is when leadership and the management of expectations are crucial.

Military culture, especially the small-unit culture, is divided into two distinct classes—those who have been in combat and those who have not. As I've mentioned earlier in this work, our civilian *and* military cultures have long lionized the individual warrior who has proved himself on the battlefield. We admire and honor those who are brave in combat; we create a kind of nobility for them. No one is decorated for restraint or proportionality on the battlefield. It's little wonder that combat experience is so prized; in many ways, it in itself is a rite of passage. Small units can become polarized by who has and who has not been in combat—in a firefight. Those who have are afforded stature. Those who are perceived to have done well in combat have both stature and influence—and often that influence can surpass seniority and military rank. Combat experience can also overshadow issues of character and right and wrong conduct. There is also the adrenaline rush that comes with risking your life, and that rush, or "combat high," that comes with trading bullets with an enemy. This sometimes-addictive element aside, in the context of the small-unit culture, I believe there also exists a status issue within our military/warrior culture. The first thing a soldier in the Army looks for on another's uniform is not his rank or unit patch, but to see if he has the Combat Infantryman Badge (CIB)—a combat action badge. To this end, most warriors and apprentice warriors want to have *been* in combat rather than *be* in combat.

Another component in the calculus of wrong battlefield conduct is the loyalty that exists within the small combat units. This, perhaps more than any factor, contributes to soldiers, marines, and special operators doing the wrong thing, or, more accurately, tolerating the wrong actions of others. Loyalty is a good thing and an essential ingredient in our warrior culture. It promotes unit integrity and trust, and it binds together those who enter the arena of mortal combat.

Indeed, it might be the single most important factor in a combat unit's effectiveness. There's more than a little truth to the contention that men fight not for their nation or for the cause, but for the guy fighting alongside them. I would go so far as to call it a necessary virtue in combat. But this loyalty cuts two ways. When someone knowingly does the wrong thing on the battlefield, who is going to stop him or report him? When my brother warrior, who has fought alongside me and has risked his life with me, gets bored and starts to harass the locals while on patrol, what do I do? I owe him a lot more than I owe some villager who may have at one time given aid and comfort to my insurgent enemy. How do I respond when, out of frustration or boredom, my battle buddy does something stupid or criminal—or both?

The loyalty thing is deeply embedded in our social fabric and certainly in our military culture. At the Naval Academy, I was recently privileged to teach some of the finest young men and women in America. The midshipmen in my classes have been in uniform for less than two years. As they are in a military-academic environment, they are not what I would call fully formed warriors. Yet they've had many hours devoted to values training, specifically the Academy Honor Concept—the equivalent in their world to the warrior code. Even at this juncture, loyalty to their classmates—to each other—can sometimes trump all other values. The Navy's core values are Honor, Courage, Commitment, and the first of these is Honor. I taught ethics, and in one of the required term papers, my midshipmen were asked to deal with a scenario in which, in an official capacity, they must choose whether to place a classmate on report for a serious conduct offense or to cover for that classmate with a lie. It's a clear and classic case of loyalty versus honor. A surprising number chose loyalty at the risk of their dismissal from the Academy. These are apprentice warriors who have shared the hardships of plebe summer and the rigors of academic and military life at a service academy—challenging to be sure, but hardly the stuff of life and death in close combat. Yet bonds have formed such that loyalty will, in some cases, win out over honor. If our best and brightest are tempted to cover up wrong behavior in a school setting, what are we to expect of our soldiers and marines whose brotherhood is forged on the battlefield?

I've also found that issues of loyalty and honor are a tricky business, and perspective on these two virtues to be an elusive thing. Academically and intuitively, honor should come first; its senior ranking comes from nearly everything we are taught. Most people understand this before they enter the military, and military training reinforces this order of priorities. We're all taught the maxim "Loyalty above all else except honor." But these words are seldom challenged until it comes to an issue of *personal* loyalty. Then it becomes difficult. I believe that those in uniform fully *know* what is right when there's a conflict between honor and loyalty. As those in uniform gain experience and maturity, these concepts become clearer, and we come to learn that loyalty is many things, including loyalty to the Constitution, the service, and the mission. But when we're younger and less experienced, loyalty to our friends is very powerful—sometimes overpowering. We may *know* what is right, but the power of peer loyalty forces us to *act* otherwise.

If there's a single factor that allows for wrong conduct in our deployed ground combat units, it is loyalty within those very units. This is what makes a consistently high standard of tactical ethics so difficult to achieve. The virtue of honor is tightly bound to the warrior ethos and right conduct on the battlefield. When honor fails, it's quite often due to the competing virtue of loyalty. Since this is an issue in the small-unit culture, any corrective action or remediation must be addressed here. And since our warriors prepare for deployment as a unit, much of the small-unit culture, certainly for the new men, is formed during the predeployment period. That is a good place to begin to look for ways to positively influence this culture and to reinforce those virtues of honor, courage, integrity, service, and (properly directed) loyalty.

It has been a relatively easy task for me to investigate military training that relates to values, the warrior ethos, character, and the moral framework that promotes good warrior conduct in the training commands. What takes place that may promote or reinforce these values in the operational units is not so easy to identify. More to the point, how good conduct is instilled in the operational units varies widely and, in many cases, is left to the discretion of the battalion- and company-level commanders. The most common deployment "increment," or unit, in the Army and the Marine Corps is the battalion. The special operators will deploy in various groups—battalion and/or team configurations that are often redistributed in smaller elements as they are scattered across the conventional battlespace in support of the conventional-battlespace commanders.

Nearly all of these units have proscribed and formatted training requirements that test their professional and physical preparation for their deployment rotation. There are schools, special training venues, and combined field-training exercises. In many cases there are multiunit, multiservice integrated certification exercises that serve as ready-for-combat credentialing. More recently these exercises and predeployment training scenarios have come to include preparation that is specific to the insurgent battlefield, including cross-cultural training and an emphasis on language and the customs of local populations. This is all to the good, but there is little time or training devoted to warrior ethics or what I would call warriorship. The training that does touch on moral issues usually relates the rules of engagement and defining the battlefield conduct that lies inside and outside of these ROE boundaries. Close attention to the physical and professional requirements for combat deployment is understandable. It's a busy time and an important time, and there are competing demands for every moment. Commanders and unit leaders want to get their troops ready for war and still give them as much time off as possible to be with their families. Within these time constraints, the moral health of the small operational unit is sometimes overlooked. Again, this is not an easy time. How do you tell a soldier or a marine returning for his third combat rotation to Iraq or Afghanistan that instead of leaving early on a Friday for some family time, he has to stay late for some core-values training or to talk about right conduct on the battlefield? The answer is, you don't.

So how *do* we provide ongoing moral conditioning for our warriors without returning to boot-camp-style lectures on ethics or mandatory discussion groups on a break during a forced conditioning march. I believe there's a need for ongoing moral conditioning, but it has to be done *in conjunction with* professional and physical training. I further believe that the "good values" of our service-component initial-training venues can only be carried to the battlespace if these values are revisited and reinforced on a regular basis in the operational units. Additionally, the messages that relate these good values have to be carefully framed and made relevant to the small-unit culture. They have to flow into the physical and professional training that small units have come to expect as required and needed battlefield prep. And this information has to be carefully nuanced if it is to address and offset the negative effects of boredom, revenge, and misplaced loyalty. Two organizations have done some good work in the area, and there's something to be gained by taking a closer look at their programs. One is a civilian training entity, Close Quarters Defense; the other is the United States Marine Corps. The balance of this chapter is devoted to their efforts in this area. First, Close Quarters Defense.

I first became aware of Close Quarters Defense, or CQD as it is more widely known, in the late 1990s while observing sailors in their advanced SEAL Qualification Training. By then CQD was an integral part of SEAL advanced and predeployment training. Close Quarters Defense was developed by Duane Dieter in the early 1980s. From an early age, Duane was interested in martial arts and devoted himself to training and to learning martial techniques, theories, and philosophies. He became a serious practitioner of the martial arts, achieving various black belts and awards. He also came to understand that these methods and disciplines were choreographed in nature and applicable only for competition and sport.

Once Duane had to defend himself in an actual assault, he realized that the methods he had so thoroughly studied were of limited use in a real fight. Seeing that he was unable to utilize those systems in which he had so diligently trained, Duane became impassioned to learn and master a skill set that could be used in actual engagement—that is, in combat. He traveled to Asia, to the origins of martial arts, with one objective: find a teacher who could train him in the art of the high-risk fight, not just a sport competition. Though he searched continuously and studied under numerous masters, nothing worked; there was no "discipline" with direct applications to a real fight. He returned to the United States in 1981 with a new objective: create a system that was based on the needs of the high-risk fight. Duane first attempted to incorporate what he had developed with sport and martial arts. However, he soon learned they were contradictory disciplines in theory and action; the integration of sport to a true fight, especially a fight for survival, in which you are defending your life or the life of another, was at counterpurpose. Duane had learned that martial arts and martial sport, though very dynamic and applicable in competition, were simply not practical in a deadly encounter. He then began to develop the techniques that were to become the CQD system. He refined the system over a period of nine years, emphasizing the integration of unarmed and armed skills, progressing from individual movement to team-centric tactics to the incorporation of armed-combatant, live-fire drills. In 1989 an NSW command requested CQD training, and from that point the system spread through word of mouth throughout the command and was formally adopted in 1997 because of its success and merit. The Navy SEALs, looking for just such a skill set, became interested in the CQD system and incorporated it into SEAL training in 1997.

So the application of martial arts to modern combat can be a contradiction in terms. Furthermore, our soldiers, marines, and special operators have great demands on their time. They have extensive and ongoing military skill sets to learn and keep current through their continuous training and deployment cycles. They haven't the time to pursue skills that are not directly applicable to the operational environment. A key advantage of CQD is that while it is a sophisticated, versatile, and highly effective skill set, the basics of this discipline can be taught in a relatively short period of time. Aside from the utility of the physical skills, and to the point of this discussion, this training also incorporates moral and spiritual values that accompany the projection of force. It's one of the few training venues I've encountered in which warrior values are fully embedded in the professional skill set and, indeed, the moral and the professional skills complement each other. Whether by design or by evolution in practice, there are some important antipirate elements embedded in CQD.

So, what is CQD and how is it taught? Of the many martial arts and self-defense techniques tried by our military special operators, why did this set of skills emerge as a useful and preferred discipline? And of special interest in this work, what is the relationship between this physical skill set and the warrior ethos?

The methodology for the training, at least within the SEAL community, is that experienced and motivated SEALs are trained and certified in CQD, and these men in turn become instructors and train their SEAL brothers. As with all military training, meaningful CQD instruction begins with good teachers. My experience is that the SEAL CQD instructors are uniformly men of character and experience who are well respected by their peers. As such, they are influential role models. It's important that the right men with the right values teach this material. Navy SEALs, like veteran soldiers and marines, are not as impressionable as recruits in boot camp. Yet true warriors understand they are always in training; there is always something new to learn. This is why advanced skills and combat-useful training such as CQD should be conducted by respected warriors capable of delivering the right physical skills as well as the right moral message. It's also important that they are known to be men of character in and out of uniform. This is the personification of the warrior ethos.

This is not a text on the virtues or capabilities of CQD, but it is important to understand the nature of this professional training and its battlefield utility in order to understand how this combat discipline relates to the ethical core of a warrior. For this reason, let's take a few minutes with the professional and physical aspects of this training. CQD is both an armed and unarmed integrated skill set, but first and foremost it's a behind-the-gun, team-centric skill set. It is designed to complement the skills of today's military warriors on the modern battlefield. Of great importance to those who have limited time to learn a range of military skills, CQD has universal application, and the initial level of instruction can be effectively taught in two weeks. The following is an excerpt from *The Finishing School*, my book about SEAL advanced training.

> "This is the way it looks, guys. It is the foundation of everything you will do this week during your Close Quarters Defense training. Notice Chief Dalton's legs—flexed, ready to quickly move forward or in any direction. His weight is on the balls of his feet, heels out. Note the position of his arms—up, and with the hard edges of this forearms and hands protecting his face and midsection. From this position he can deflect blows, absorb blows, and protect his vital areas. It's called the spring-stance, power-point position. Ready, Chief?"

> Dalton nods. Chief Ray Dalton is not a big man as far as Navy SEALs go, but Instructor Jack Meyers, a hefty first class petty officer, is—about six-two three and 215 pounds. He walks around Dalton and delivers a series of vicious kicks to his legs and torso. Then he shoves him a few times and kicks him again. Dalton flexes and shuffles his feet in staccato fashion and absorbs the blows. He pops back to the power-point stance like a spring-loaded snake, coiled, ready to strike. Class 2-02 is glued to the drama.

> "The body can take a lot of punishment. Now, the chief here will have a few bruises and welts from all this, but notice he didn't go down; he's still in the fight, ready to project his power . . . "

This is day one of Close Quarters Defense training in the Navy SEAL Qualification Course. The initial CQD course begins with the basic defense posture. From this first day of instruction, the training will move quickly to individual unarmed movements. By the second week, the SEAL candidates will be immersed in sophisticated, team-orientated, fully armed confrontations. Along the way, they are challenged physically, mentally, morally, and emotionally. CQD is all about managing and channeling aggression, and the tools that allow this aggression to "flow" in a lethal environment. It's about dominating one's space in a hostile confrontation and the controlled ability to absorb, deflect, and project power. It's also about restraint and the personal responsibility a warrior has for the power he projects. A true warrior has a duty and an obligation to develop a firm moral platform from which to project power.

Structurally, CQD training is presented in multilevel increments with each level of training lasting two weeks. Training can be tailored to meet operational requirements. The skills learned in these courses provide the warrior with an integrated tactical skill set that has proved successful in a range of lethal and nonlethal situations, and in compliant and hostile environments. This progressive, interdisciplinary training imbues the operator/warrior with a heightened sense of mind, body, and spirit. While the training is progressive and cumulative, the initial two weeks can greatly extend the reach of the warrior. In my book *Down Range: Navy SEALs in the War on Terrorism*, a SEAL had this to say about a close-quarters fight he was involved in. He had trained for only two weeks in CQD.

> "I came through the door into a room and this Iraqi, one of the target's bodyguards, came at me with a knife. Now, under normal conditions, that knife would have earned him a bullet. You never let a guy get close to you with a lethal weapon—if you can help it. But, at a glance, I saw a woman and some kids behind him. . . . So I let this Iraqi come at me and took him out with a barrel strike. He went down like a sack of cement. We moved on through the house and found the guy we came to get. The bodyguard with the knife was still out cold when we hustled the target out of there.

"With the CQD training behind me, it was all instinct, and yet it felt like it was almost in slow motion. It was like 'Okay, he's earned a bullet, shoot him—oops, can't shoot him; Mom and kids behind him—barrel strike to the head.' It was a chain of decisions, but they happened instantly. And I'll tell you something else. It really feels good to have done the right thing—to have made a good call. If I hadn't had the ability to recognize the potential harm to noncombatants and the ability to take him down without lethal force, I'd have had no choice but to shoot him and risk harm to the others. I wouldn't have minded shooting him, but my training gave me a better option—certainly better for the noncombatants and, as it turned out, better for him."

Regarding CQD, a host of techniques and devices had to be developed to support this training for the real-world fight. Technique-wise, they range from basic individual movement to situational-awareness drills designed to accelerate threat recognition and reduce reaction time. One such technique developed by Duane is the Hooded Box Drill. This involves a dramatic, repetitive scenario designed to challenge the operator's response and sharpen his military and moral reaction skills. Picture this: A fully armed SEAL—full body armor, helmet, M4 rifle, radio, associated operational equipment, sidearm, and so on—stands in the middle of a padded room. A four-sided curtain has been lowered from the ceiling and covers his head and shoulders—the hood. When the hood is snatched up, he is confronted with a situation. It could be a man in Arab dress with a map asking for directions. It could be a woman with a pistol in the folds of her robe. It could be an American soldier trying to subdue an Arab youth. It could be two merchants arguing. It could be *anything*. Usually it's a lethal situation, but not always. The game, and the art, is to assess and react, professionally and proportionally. The Hooded Box Drill may involve a single warrior or two of them working in a buddy team. It's an adrenaline rush just to watch it play out. Nearly all of these scenarios are drawn from recent combat experience. What makes this training valuable and unique is that it teaches useful combat skills while challenging the warrior to be moral and proportional at the same time.

Since much of CQD training is full-on adversarial combat, specially designed protective equipment is a must; lethal blows are taken and given. Techniques may be taught without protection or at slow speed to demonstrate form or proper application, but drills are conducted at full speed. To make this training as real as possible, a great deal of time, attention, and multiday course work is devoted to the schooling of training partners. CQD training is not orchestrated movement; it's fighting to the death. Tactical Role Players™ are essential to the process of developing CQD warriors. When a Navy SEAL in Iraq takes an insurgent down with a barrel or hand strike or immobilizes a detainee in a fast-moving, lethal setting, it's something he's done many times and in many different environments during his CQD training. And this training requires competent, aggressive, and well-armored training partners.

Before we get to the moral and ethical aspects of this training, one additional perspective on the physical. Warriors in combat require a firm physical platform from which to deliver their power. Simply being in shape or mastering the skills is not enough. Duane Dieter has incorporated Operational Physical Training™ as an integral part of the discipline. This is a physical regime that conditions and hardens the body to better handle CQD and to build specific physical capabilities and reserves to sustain a warrior in a close-quarters fight to the death. As an example, hand and weapon strikes are fundamental components of CQD. During OPTs the operator is commanded to activate these skills while in all positions: standing, ground, and transitional. Push ups in themselves have no combat utility. However, push-ups done on the knife-edges of one's hands, or one-armed push-ups, done by the operator while remaining in the "up" position and striking the ground or mat rapidly with the palm of each hand—left, right, left, right—toughens the hands and conditions the warrior for repeated and explosive hand strikes. This kind of conditioning builds muscle memory and reminds the practitioner that this is warrior business—that delivering physical blows are a part of it.

Above all, however, CQD training promotes a unique mind-set. The training demands an integration of the professional and the physical with the ethical—the moral platform from which a warrior delivers his power. Perhaps the most important "skill" of this tactical system is not really a skill at all. It's the concept of the Inner Warrior. When Duane Dieter and his instructors teach (in class and by example) the precepts of the Inner Warrior to CQD students, they make it clear that personal development and balance in one's life are *essential* to the warrior's ability to perform in the fight—that is, on the battlefield. But they don't stop there. The Inner Warrior curriculum also teaches respect, humility, and compassion. Since to fight is to risk death, life itself is often the prize of victory. The moral edge a warrior derives from a deep-seated commitment to his family, community, and nation, and those who support him, cannot be underestimated. Today our military warriors often carry this fight—our fight—to the "true believers" of other faiths, so they must therefore be professionally, physically, *and* morally conditioned for battle. Implicit in this is that if a warrior is to be moral, which adds to his power, then he must be honorable. Both on and off the battlefield, a warrior must protect his honor—much as he cares for his equipment and the welfare of his brother warriors. The notion that character, personal honor, patriotism, and restraint are tools that extend a warrior's power are reinforced continuously in this training.

A final thought regarding CQD and, for want of a better term, "right-conduct conditioning" in training for the moral fight. It involves what SEALs call "finding the dial," and it relates to being able to control the level of aggression—to dial it up or down. In this work I've often referred to the concept of proportionality—the proportional use of force. The SEALs in CQD training call it the dial. Several years ago I was sitting in on a final briefing conducted by a SEAL CQD trainer. He was addressing a SEAL platoon that had just completed an increment of CQD training. Here's one last excerpt from *The Finishing School*.

"Remember, you have to control the situation and minimize the threat. Take charge. Don't let some badass minimize you. Dial it up when you have to, and dial it down when it is appropriate. If you can control the threat, then you may avoid having to kill somebody who may not need to die. Don't forget, you are responsible when you send those rounds downrange and turn someone's lights out. And you will have to answer for the action you take. That's a big-time responsibility. With this training, you may have a better option. With this training, you may be able to control a situation and not have to take a life. Make it their choice. But hear me on this one: If a bad guy threatens you or your teammates and won't have it any other way, you shoot him and keep shooting him until he's dead. Don't hesitate. . . . They get what they deserve—no more, no less."

This idea of the proportional dispensing of violence ties in professional military skill with moral action. The notion of including warrior virtue and restraint in combat preparation can have an important influence when applied to what constitutes right conduct in the battlespace. When proportionality and restraint are a part of the conditioning process, there is little room for wrong conduct that may result from boredom or revenge. These values also act as a buttress to negative contemporary social influences. As discussed in the previous chapter, there is ample opportunity for the imprinting of gratuitous violence in America. The negative societal influences are still at work, even for those actively serving in the military. Our off-duty soldiers can still find bad messages in media-generated violence or at a mixed martial arts competition or in a social setting. Regarding the latter, little takes place in the bars of our cities or around our military bases that would support warrior values or right warrior conduct. It is not the objective of this work to find fault with American culture, nor is it the objective of the military to create warrior-monks. But it's a simple fact that there are limited recreational outlets and social activities that promote the warrior ethos, just as there are seemingly limited rewards afforded in our popular culture for those who practice restraint.

This is where concepts like CQD's Inner Warrior become valuable and instructional. These concepts teach that there is virtue in right conduct *away* from the battlefield. They not only promote right conduct and good judgment in combat, but they lead to professional and physical superiority in combat. Full-on mortal combat is emotional and demanding business. So is the more routine, day-to-day conduct of operations in the battlespace—activities such as training local police, engaging in vehicle and foot patrols, and conducting civil-affairs functions. Warriors who see virtue and nobility in their calling are more often than not men who follow a warrior ethos off duty and in garrison. The practice of right conduct when they are not in uniform or in an off-duty status makes it a great deal easier to do the right thing in battle. To use a sports analogy, a good basketball player is one who moves well away from the ball. It's the same with soldiering and warriorship. How a man lives his life is highly predictive of how he will perform as a warrior. Few callings are as demanding as that of our deployed ground combatants; they must draw strength and perspective from their nonworking environment. I give a lot of credit to Duane Dieter for his pioneering work in the marriage of physical and professional skill sets with the moral and ethical continuum of a complete warrior. The physical and professional skills in themselves are valuable. The moral and ethical skills are essential. The role of the Inner Warrior in CQD is outlined in Appendix V.

The goal of CQD's Inner Warrior is to help our special operators bring spirituality, physical conditioning, focused aggression, and professional training to the fight. CQD challenges the warrior to use the right blend of these skills to dominate his battlespace. It also becomes a great force multiplier when a warrior, young or old, takes control of the forces that guide his inner self. I've asked a number of CQD students what they learned from their training—what they felt the takeaways were. Most told me that what they learned about themselves and the kind of warrior they wanted to be far outweighed the physical and the professional skills. These concepts are important in and of themselves, but more so as they provide a tie-in of values learned during basic/initial training to that moment when an individual warrior steps onto the battlefield.

Regarding the Navy SEALs and their approach to the ethical and moral component of warrior development, there was a time in the late 1990s and just after the attacks of 9/11 that the only formal, sustained training in character and the warrior ethos was provided by Close Quarters Defense.

The United States Marine Corps also sees value-based conduct as an essential part of the warrior ethos. In comparison to Close Quarters Defense, the Marine Corps is a very big organization. When compared to its sister services, the Corps is small. Since it is an expeditionary force and its integrated-arms posture is limited, the Marines can promote an internal ethos that supports their culture—a culture that holds that every marine is a rifleman. Compared to the Army, the Navy, and the Air Force, the Marines have a higher tooth-to-tail ratio—a higher number of combatants when compared to those who serve in combat-support roles. In short, it's a smaller, leaner force that lends itself to a top-to-bottom warrior ethos. Because it is essentially a ground-combat force, with most of its auxiliary elements dedicated to ground-combat support, the Marines have given a great deal of time and thought to warriorship and right conduct on the battlefield. I don't mean that the other services are less moral or less attentive to duty than the Marines, but not even the Army has the luxury of the limited and focused ground-combat role enjoyed by the Marines. To be honest about it, the Marines understand the role of honor in warfighting, and they put a lot of stock in the warrior-ethos conditioning.

Aside from the cultlike once-a-marine, always-a-marine brotherhood, the Corps does a number of things that collectively promote right conduct on the battlefield. These relate to recognition of ongoing values training, institutional training venues, leadership, and a pride of service that is highly parochial. Let's begin with ongoing values.

As a combat arm, the Marines recognize and acknowledge that attention to values and a defined warrior ethic—centered on those same Marine Corps Core Values that are all but force-fed to young recruits—has to be sustained. The Marines have embraced a concept of "Value Based Training" that they define as a method or "delivery system" by which they promote the Marine Corps Core Values of Honor, Courage, and Commitment to *all* marines—during basic training (what they call entry-level training) and beyond. Past the twelve-week basic-training period and the core-values training associated with this initial training, the Marines use the term "reinforcement training" to denote their follow-on, value-based training. This is the training that takes place at the School of Infantry and other Marine professional military schools. Basically this reinforcement training is to keep the issues of warriorship, ethos, and the Marine Corps Core Values topical—to keep them a part of that continuum which carries the young marine through his postbasic training and into his operational unit. It directs the command levels in these advanced schools to use guided discussion, recommended professional reading, and mentoring activity to keep the combat-bound marine in touch with his core values. It also directs command attention to the development and education of designated guided discussion leaders. Basically it's an attempt to burnish some of the value-based luster the new marines bring with them from their basic training.

From the reinforcement training of the advanced and specialty schools, the Marines support value-based training in their permanent duty stations in the form of what they call sustainment training. As the term implies, this training is designed to sustain the Marine Corps Core Values in the operational commands. It does this by keeping all that the core values demand current in the mind of each marine. Sustainment training seeks to embed the core values through leadership training, an expanded reading list, mentorship, and an association of these practices with professional common-skills training. Another goal of sustainment training is to promote an internalizing of these core values up and down the chain of command. All of this is an attempt to keep Marine Corps Core Values in front of the troops on a recurring basis and to promote a continuum of these values from basic training to battlefield.

The Marines are very rigid in their methodology of their core-values training; in the case of reinforcement and sustainment training, there are programs, directives, instructions, and the like. From this nonmarine's perspective, I believe it is a good attempt on the part of the senior Marine leadership to remind junior marines that they are just that—they are marines, and that their individual conduct reflects on a sacred and noble organization called the United States Marine Corps. Sometimes I think the Marine Corps took a page from the controlling ideology of the Catholic Church. The church promotes good works and right conduct because it is right and good in the sight of God, but there's always that strong measure of guilt for giving in to the weakness of the flesh. In the case of the Marines, there is a similar measure of guilt that comes if your conduct tarnishes the image of the Corps. This guilt-induced restraint may not apply to all marines and not in every instance, but marines are continually reminded that theirs is a proud heritage. Young marines are also reminded that they did not earn this noble history—they inherited it. As new marines, they may by their conduct add to that proud tradition or soil it. By this association, there is the shame and guilt that accompanies wrong conduct.

While the Corps formally understands and encourages ongoing ethical refinement of marines through sustainment training, I'm aware of no set requirement or fixed, formal course work in values or warrior ethos for units preparing for the battlefield. Instead, that responsibility is left to the deploying units, usually at the battalion level. In practice, battalion commanders give this job to their company commanders, who encourage their platoon leaders—officers and senior sergeants—to ensure that their marines know what they can and cannot do in the operational theater. So the moral health conditioning of those marines headed for battle is put on the leadership at the platoon level, which is not a bad place for it. The Marines take great pains to screen and train their junior officers and in the selection and training of senior enlisted marines, and they hold them accountable for Marine battlefield conduct. There's not the time nor space here to go into that leadership training, but I feel I'm on solid ground by saying that it's some of the best and most comprehensive junior-leader training in our military. At the platoon and squad level, value and ethos training in the Marine Corps is built on a leadership model that empowers these key small-unit leaders. I've spoken with a number of these junior leaders. All of them acknowledge an obligation to get this message to their troops, but they also say that there is no formal requirement or set methodology to do this. Each one that I spoke with had a different take on what should be done and how they went about this important duty.

The company commanders, platoon leaders, and sergeants I interviewed seem to use a blend of personal examples, lessons learned, experiences drawn from mentors, and an expectation of right conduct based on the Marine Corps Core Values. Many use sessions on theater-specific rules of engagement to get their message across. At this stage of our engagement in Afghanistan and Iraq, there is no shortage of incidents and investigations that serve as examples of what not to do.

One Marine first lieutenant told me how much he was taken with one of his mentor's perspectives on a combat leader's duty. This involved three imperatives: be prepared for anything, win always, and return your marines to society better than when you took them into battle. Implicit in the latter imperative is to bring them home having done nothing that they are ashamed of or will cause them psychological damage or post-traumatic stress disorder. "To that end," this young Marine officer told me, "we talked about that a lot. Making sure of targets, full compliance with the ROEs, avoiding indiscriminate shooting, and what it means to take life. We talked about having to live the rest of our lives with what we do in Afghanistan and Iraq. The older guys got it right away. It took a while, but the younger guys got it as well. It's not always easy to get across to some nineteen-year-old PFC or lance corporal that he has ethical responsibilities—that he can be legally and ethically responsibility for conduct in a firefight.

You do your best; you keep talking it up, during training and in the battlespace."

"A lot of what I do is serve as a translator for what is right and wrong—what is acceptable conduct and what is unacceptable conduct," another junior Marine leader told me. "Some battalions have the JAGs [judge advocate generals—that is, military lawyers] speak to the troops about what is and is not legal regarding the ROEs. This means nothing to many young marines. I had to translate those ROEs, and all issues relating to conduct to my marines, in words they could understand. Many of them don't really understand it unless you give them examples. I also had to make it plain as to what I expected and what were the consequences of wrong conduct. It's tough love; I told them I'd hammer them if they were out of line. We've been at this war a while, and we've all lost friends and buddies. Revenge is an issue I always had to be aware of and keep my squad leaders aware of. A lot of young marines and not-so-young marines are waiting for any chance to give some of it back. It was my job to channel that aggression and emotion within the legal and moral boundaries. You never know just how powerful the issue of revenge is unless you spend time with your troops. I'd take every opportunity to get one-on-one with my troops—to get to know what they were thinking. If you know what the troops are thinking and talking about, you can sometimes head off problems."

Yet another Marine officer had this to say about leading a Marine platoon in combat; it had to do with segregating talk and action—talking the talk and walking the walk. "You have to be careful what the guys are saying and what they're doing. They all talk trash—it comes from the movies, TV, rap music, you name it. It's the way things are, and most of it is just talk. Some of it is pretty graphic, and it makes you wonder what the hell they're really thinking. I found my senior marines could talk trash with the best of them, but they knew right action from wrong action; they knew right from wrong because we talked about it seriously, and I trusted them to do the right thing. My concerns were with some of the younger marines. It took them a while to separate the talk from the walk—what was expected of them in the way of maturity and right conduct on the battlefield. Once we got into the battlespace, it was a matter of keeping the issues of right conduct current with the changing tactical situation. And I had to learn this. Talk is just talk. I had to get past some of the trash talk, and really understand what they were really thinking. Most of my marines want to do the right thing, and they do the right thing. They just don't always talk like it."

I found this to be much the same in speaking with special operations team, platoon, and task element leaders. Ethos and values training during their predeployment work-up was largely left to them and their senior enlisted leaders. Many told me that most battlefield-conduct training centered on understanding and implementing the rules of engagement.

Back to the Marines. The issues of right conduct and how conduct requirements change, especially on the insurgent battlefield, are deeply embedded in the Marines. The Corps sees itself as a force that fights the small wars, and each of these small wars, even when they become medium-sized ones, is different from the last one. It's part of the Marines' flexible, expeditionary-warfare charter, and they have to be ready to do it all. As evidence of their readiness to do this, the Corps created something called the Three Block War concept. This holds that in the space of three city blocks, marines can be expected to be passing out MREs (meals ready to eat) and soccer balls on one block, patrolling to maintain an easy peace on the second, and engaged in an intense firefight on the third. Perhaps not a bad way to look at modern insurgent warfare.

For a good perspective on Marine Corps culture and leadership, I recommend two books: *Generation Kill* and *One Bullet Away*. *Generation Kill*, by Evan Wright, is a talented journalist's embedded account with a Marine Corps reconnaissance platoon in close combat during the early days of our invasion of Iraq and the early days of the war. Wright does a decent job of documenting today's small-unit culture as it applies to a single Marine platoon engaged in combat. It also documents just how devastating modern maneuver warfare operations can be to a civilian population. *One Bullet Away*, by Nate

Fick, is a Marine platoon leader's personal story, one told with skill, intelligence, and emotion. It tells of the responsibility and leadership challenges of a combat leader charged with taking the current generation of marines to war—and bringing them home intact, physically and psychologically. The perspective these two books offer is unique; they are about the *same platoon*. For those of us who are interested in battlefield conduct and the generation we are putting in the field, they form an invaluable anthology of the current fight. Both books also speak to the importance of competent combat leadership and the risk to the men in combat if it is lacking.

In summary, both Close Quarters Defense and the Marine Corps have something to offer here. CQD ties the warrior ethos to a specific tactical skill set and promotes this as a package—the moral supports the physical and the professional, and all three integrate to make a more complete and effective warrior in battle. CQD also instills the notion that a complete warrior is one who practices virtue at home, in garrison, and in his personal life. Right conduct *away* from the battlefield will help a warrior prevail *on* the battlefield. This takes the old adage that you "fight like you train" a step further. You succeed in the fight as you succeed in life. In the case of the Marines, theirs is a leadership model. They count on their junior leaders to know the Marine Corps Core Values and to be able to keep those values before their marines during their precombat training and in the battlespace. The Marines also put a great deal of faith in their history and the nobility of their culture. It's for the junior leaders to see that the current Marine small-unit culture conforms to all that is good in the Marine Corps, and that conduct in the platoons and squads is in keeping with that good. Both CQD and the Marines seek to keep good personal values and the warrior ethos as a part of the skill base that a complete warrior needs when he enters combat.

CHAPTER SIX

Battlefield ROEs (Rules of Ethics)

U p to this point, I have tried to define some of the problems—the challenges to right conduct on the battlefield. There are the negative influences in society, the corrosive influence of the pirates, and the moral challenges of the insurgent battlespace. The previous chapter explored what Duane Dieter offers in Close Quarters Defense to integrate the warrior ethos into one tactical set of skills. I also covered what our smallest service component, the Marine Corps, does to shore up the moral health of its troops for ground combat in the way of sustainment training and strong leadership. Next I will explore some rules or guidelines that might be useful in evolving a better tactical ethos and reducing wrong conduct on the modern battlefield. But first I would like to discuss who might find this information useful and when they might find it useful.

It stands to reason that everyone in uniform, from senior battlefield commanders to the foot soldiers in the squads and platoons, stands to profit from right conduct in battle. All share a universal goal: to prepare appropriately for the fight, conduct themselves in battle with courage and virtue, win the fight, and return with honor. But good intentions do not always translate into good conduct. It is my hope that this material will be useful for both senior commanders and junior warriors, but I think it is particularly suited for the junior and noncommissioned officers—those charged with leadership at the company, platoon, and squad levels. This is where the fighting gets done, and the leadership at these levels will ultimately determine conduct on the battlefield—appropriate or inappropriate.

These junior leaders are the company commanders, platoon commanders, first sergeants, teams sergeants, and squad leaders. The commissioned officers will most often step into the traces of ground-combat leadership with a unit that is a standing entity, one that will have a combat history and includes a cadre of veterans and men new to the unit like themselves. This new officer may or may not be a combat veteran himself. It doesn't matter; he is still responsible for seeing that the actions of those under him are appropriate—that their conduct is within the standards, both on and off the battlefield. A senior enlisted leader may be new to the unit or may have been promoted from that unit's ranks to a leadership position. Either way, his position as an enlisted leader charges him with the responsibility for the conduct of those under him. All military leaders, as they assume command or step into their leadership role, must assert their leadership within the moral framework of their unit, and communicate to their subordinates what they will and will not tolerate in the way of conduct, both on and off the battlefield. This brings us to when these rules might be applied to best advantage.

Since these rules serve to guide leaders in managing the conduct of their operational units, a good place to impose them is when the unit begins its work-up for deployment rotation. This may not be true for each and every ground-combat unit, but most begin training as a unit, a team, or a deployment package, and they will rotate into the battlespace as a unit. For many of our units headed for the battlespace, the deployment package is a battalion or battalion-sized unit, but usually no smaller than a company. Prior to the deployment work-up or training period, the companies, task units, teams, platoons, and so on undergo a re-formation or realignment as both troops and leaders rotate out and their replacements rotate in. Sometimes there's a strong corps of veterans, and the unit coalesces around their experience. Other times there are a number of new men and precious few veterans. Usually there is a new officer, and sometimes there is new senior enlisted leadership. In any case, roles, responsibilities, policies, and expectations within the unit are defined or redefined as the unit puts the last rotation behind it and begins to prepare for the next. One thing is certain: each of these deployment-bound, ground-combat components, especially the squads and platoons, are minicultures. If the culture within that combat unit is righteous and compatible, disciplined and well led, then it will perform well on deployment. If the culture is otherwise, the unit is a candidate for problems. Good leadership and the promotion of right conduct are important anytime in the rotation cycle, but it is particularly appropriate as the units begin training for deployment, especially combat deployment.

The following guidelines are meant more in the way of suggestions, even though I offer them up as my ROEs—Rules of Ethics. My intent is that this information will be useful, especially for you small-unit combat leaders going into harm's way. My hope would be that you could take this list and tuck it into your kit as a helpful reference. In whatever manner this information might be used, I trust that it may serve you well. Good luck on your battlefield.

1. *The Expectation Rule.* Soldiers, marines, and special operators in a ground-combat unit cannot perform up to expectations unless those expectations are clearly defined. This applies to physical and professional preparation for battle, but most especially to the ethical preparation—that is, preparing to confront issues of right and wrong conduct. Early in the deployment-preparation cycle, small-unit leaders need to communicate on a recurring basis what is expected regarding good conduct, both in garrison and when the unit gets to the battlespace. It must be made clear that right conduct is in keeping with a true warrior ethos; the statutory rules of engagement must be observed. Each ground-combat leader must also clearly define what constitutes unacceptable conduct and describe the consequences of wrongdoing.

Predeployment is a busy time; it always is. Just as junior leaders make time for professional and physical training, they must also make time for moral training. Junior combat leaders *must* ensure that their men know what is and is not right conduct, and these expectations must be unambiguous.

2. *The Proximity Rule*. This is like the Expectation Rule, only it's much more subtle. The bottom line is that it's leadership by example. Soldiers, marines, and special operators closely watch their lieutenants and noncommissioned officers. How they conduct themselves is critical. By extension, the Proximity Rule holds that what a combat leader tolerates in his presence is critical. In small ground-combat units, leadership can be bottom up, so what that PFC or lance corporal tolerates in the combat leader's presence is critical as well. The collective moral content of a unit is highly influenced by what the leaders of that unit, those with rank *and* those without, tolerate in their presence. Often, it's a quiet intolerance. It can simply be a comment in a conversation, such as "Y'know, that kind of thing just doesn't work with me," or quietly excusing yourself and moving away when the discussion runs to the dysfunctional. Our individual characters are defined by our actions and by what we allow to go on around us—what we tolerate in our presence. It's the same with the character and culture of a small ground-combat unit. Its collective tolerance for wrong conduct defines the health of its warrior ethos.

3. *The Battle-Buddy Rule*. Nearly everyone needs someone close at hand that can serve as a confidant and a sounding board—someone to share information with, knowing it will remain between them. This information could be tactical as well as moral: What just happened? How could we have done this better? What's just ahead? This is especially true for junior leaders on the battlefield. In a platoon-sized organization, it's important that the platoon officer and the senior enlisted leader(s) have this relationship. This does not sever the junior-senior command relationship, but instead promotes communication. It allows key small-unit leaders to decide what is right and to make corrections when things are not right. Moving down the hierarchy, every junior sergeant or squad

leader needs this kind of informal point of contact—either with another squad leader or his platoon sergeant or team sergeant. For the troops, that battle buddy is essential. Sometimes when a soldier is about to move in a bad direction, that restraining hand on his shoulder that says, "Hold on, let's think about this," is all it takes. This informal kind of mutual support is set in place when small-unit leaders say, "Guys, let's be looking out for each other out there." This means that they should watch each other's backs, tactically and morally.

4. *The Alcohol Tolerance Rule (in garrison)*. In the military, alcohol is the drug of choice, and most servicemen drink. Some of them drink to excess, probably in the same proportion as civilians of the same age group. This is a tough one, and merits the close attention of junior combat leaders. A few beers after the training day *can be* good for a squad or platoon. A lot of beers in a bar late at night *is* a very bad thing for a squad or platoon. I've spoken with young warriors who tell of the late-night phone calls that "summon" them to the team bar. The good ones don't like these calls, and their wives hate them. It means the pirates are trying to take charge. The rule here is not specific, but it does require that the unit leaders, senior and junior, don't allow their culture to get to this point. I knew a SEAL platoon chief who, in the course of a predeployment work-up, always took his platoon out to a bar after a hard day's training for more than a few beers. "I make sure we have a designated driver, and I keep the pitchers coming. And I watch the new men closely. I want to know who drinks, who drinks to excess, and how it affects them." Then what? I asked him. "Then I tell them who can and cannot drink, and what their limits are." You can do that? I asked. "In my platoons I can and do. The guys know what I expect of them—what goes and what does not go. That's how it is. And when we go on deployment and I say there is no drinking, they'll know it's not an option." I don't put this example forward as a template, but to demonstrate that small-unit leaders have to understand the effects of drinking

on their troops—both as a group and as individuals. For some, drinking is recreation or an outlet; for others, it is an addiction. There is a time to insist on abstinence, and a combat deployment is one of them. It's part of the warrior's calling.

5. *The Alcohol Tolerance Rule (in the battlespace)*. Because alcohol can be a problem, it merits a second rule. Stated simply, there is *no* drinking in the battlespace. General Order #1, originated in November 1990 before the First Gulf War, prohibits the consumption of alcohol in an active theater. The use of alcohol and pornography and the taking of war trophies/souvenirs are not allowed. These prohibitions are particularly important in our current role as a counterinsurgent force in Muslim nations. Any junior leader who tolerates alcohol and believes he can manage the issue, or has his own modification to General Order #1, is wrong and in violation. Alcohol and/or drugs and duty on the modern battlefield simply do not mix. Looking back to my time in Vietnam, there were a number of things that cost us that war, and I believe alcohol was one of them. Today's small-unit leaders should never encourage any leeway; they must insist on compliance with General Order #1. During predeployment training, good leaders will promote the expectation that there will be no drinking in the battlespace.

6. *The Boredom Rule*. On the battlefield, and especially on the insurgent battlefield, boredom can be as deadly to the mission as an improvised explosive device (IED) is to your person. Units headed for the battlespace prepare in every way they can for combat. Combat leaders are remiss if they don't do all in their power to ready their men physically, professionally, and morally for battle. Along with this comes the expectation of combat, including the inclination to seek out combat as a validation of that preparation. It's the currency of our warrior culture. There is no substitute for success on the battlefield. Since we must always win, we must always train to win. But how do you prepare for boredom? What do you do when you've diligently prepared for battle and there is no

fight? Or, as is often the case in an insurgency, what if the preparation and the expectation is for close combat, and the mission calls for the training of local security forces or endless patrols to maintain an uneasy peace? This is difficult for the veterans who recall, perhaps with rose-colored hindsight, the rush of combat. It's difficult for the new men who long to be true combat-veteran warriors. The small-unit leadership must deal with these unmet expectations. Officers and NCOs must refocus the unit culture on the mission, and not allow the boredom or the lack of tactical challenges to degenerate into wrong conduct on the battlefield—conduct that can range from a wrongful shooting to demeaning treatment of the locals.

7. *The Recognition Rule.* All small units, especially those involved in ground combat, are tightly meshed minicultures. They are essentially a pack, and a pack is highly influenced by the strong personalities within it. This can lead to an informal hierarchy. There is the military hierarchy, and there is that which occurs with the emergence of natural leaders and individual agents of influence. The hierarchy established by military rank and the one based on strong personality may or not be one and the same. The emergence of natural leaders in the combat unit can be exceptionally positive. Nothing is more beneficial or more welcomed by a small-unit leader than for a veteran or two, or even a new trooper, to emerge as an effective and positive role model. When those in the ranks stand up for what is right, they help to form intolerance for what is not right. The moral health of the unit benefits. Lieutenants and senior sergeants must be quick to recognize and encourage this kind of bottom-up leadership. On the other side of the equation, they must be quick to recognize and neutralize the men in their units who promote negative values and wrong conduct.

8. *The Intolerance Rule.* Units with high marks in physical skill and professional accomplishment can nevertheless develop poor moral health; one or more pirates in the minority can spread dis-

ease within the group. I strongly suspect that a soldier, marine, or special operator who chooses to become a pirate and do the wrong thing emerges due to the dysfunctional and violent aspects of our culture, which may finally burn through the warrior imprinting of his military training. Or the wrong conduct and breaking of rules may be purely an issue of twisted values or some misplaced need to control others. Bad conduct could also result from a need to force confrontation or to seek thrills—or simply be an antidote for boredom. Whatever the reason, this influence needs to be exorcised, and quickly. A ground-combat leader may have neither the time nor the opportunity for counseling or punishment. The situation calls for the immediate segregation of the rogue individual. This might precede an administrative or bad-conduct discharge. Summarily removing a troublemaker can be dramatic and effective; excommunication works. Separation sends a strong message to the pack within the small combat unit, and may cause those influenced by the exiled pirate to realign their thinking. Most men in the ranks want to do the right thing. Removing temptation and negative influence reinforces others to also do the right thing.

In the rare case when a platoon officer and/or a senior enlisted leader becomes a pirate and the source of wrong conduct, it's the job of the company and battalion commanders to correct it, quickly and severely. This also applies to all small-unit leaders who, through inaction, incompetence, or compliance, tolerate wrong action within their ground-combat units.

9. *The Loyalty Rule.* There is a saying for this: Loyalty above all else except honor. This is easy to say, but in many ways it's difficult to put into practice. Loyalty is perhaps the strongest collective emotion within the small ground-combat unit. It binds men together for collective effort in a lethal environment. It's also very difficult to turn off when it fails to serve the military objectives of the unit—specifically, when a brother-in-arms does something wrong. What do members of the platoon or squad mates do when one of their own, perhaps the bravest and heretofore the best of them, repeatedly does

the wrong thing? How long does the group tolerate this? When do the men put a stop to it, or at what point do they join in this wrong conduct? This is when honor and loyalty are in direct conflict, and it can be an emotional Rubicon for a young Army PFC or Marine lance corporal. A situation like this forces a young warrior to judge between what he has known is right since the day he donned a uniform and the loyalty he has for a brother warrior. When the collective ethic is right, bad conduct gets corrected at the troop level—by peer intolerance of wrong action. A wrong act is talked about and identified as something that's wrong, and the offender is placed under the scrutiny of his brother warriors so he does not repeat it. If peer intolerance is not enough, then it's up to the individual warrior to violate the bonds of peer loyalty and take it up the chain of command. There's no other way—loyalty above all else except honor.

Small-unit leaders must make it unmistakably clear to their men that wrong action on the battlefield is a form of disloyalty—to their nation, to their service, to their team brothers, and to those fallen warriors whose honor they stain. Junior leaders coming into a unit and/or new to combat may find this a difficult task, but they need to understand that it is an imperative one. Wrong conduct committed or condoned by veteran troops is especially corrosive. Nonetheless, a junior combat leader must never allow a subordinate's battlefield experience to be a substitute for a junior leader's moral authority—*never*. No level of combat experience, or lack thereof, can relieve a leader of his role as a moral agent.

10. *The Righteous Rule*. This rule can govern, mitigate, and/or override the first nine of these rules. It allows that the "fix," or correction, for wrong conduct on the battlefield is not all that difficult. And it's very like the Intolerance Rule. There are, however, two prerequisites to this rule. First, a lieutenant or a senior noncommissioned officer must have first put moral and ethical conduct above all else—have made it job one. Second, he must have the courage of his convictions and follow those convictions to a righteous conclusion. It helps if the company commander and the battalion com-

mander share his convictions, but that does not relieve the leaders at the platoon and squad level of this duty. The Righteous Rule says that anyone who deviates from the standards of right moral conduct *will* be summarily removed from the unit. The wrongdoer will be sent packing. In garrison, this means assigned to other duties; in the battlespace, he will be sent home—*in shame*.

This approach makes for immediate corrective action. Preparing troops physically and professionally for battle takes months. If they are lacking in these areas, training time can usually be found to correct these deficiencies. Morally, the troops *know* what is expected of them. Ongoing sustainment and reinforcement training can keep those issues and values current within the course of their physical and professional battlefield preparation. But when bad conduct becomes a part of the small-unit culture, that culture is broken, and very little can be done in the way of lectures or punishments or reasoning to get the "unit train" back on acceptable "moral rails." This is not an issue of training time; it's an issue of moral will. Leaders or instigators of wrong or dysfunctional conduct need to be publicly humiliated and sent away.

Regarding the application of the Righteous Rule, I fully understand that there are some administrative and legal issues associated with the "firing" of a soldier, marine, or special operator that can be formidable. It must be done with a great deal of circumspection. Yet I believe that when a warrior has been clearly identified as an agent of moral misconduct and negative influence, he has truly achieved leper status and *must* be sent away. I would offer a caveat to this kind of small-unit surgery. The good lieutenant and the good sergeant who consider this step must look into the heart of their wayward brother. To paraphrase Dr. Martin Luther King Jr., they must judge him by the content of his character. Just because the soldier, marine, or special operator talks trash, listens to rap music, watches professional wrestling, and has weird tattoos does *not* in itself make him morally unsuitable. Judge him by his character, his actions, his influence (positive or negative) on his brother warrior, and his contribution to the mission. I've seen it done right. The excommunication of a single pirate can save a platoon—it can even save an entire company.

As a final thought and perhaps some advice to senior leaders—battalion commanders, brigade commanders, general officers, and up: *listen* to your company and platoon officers. Senior enlisted leaders at the battalion and brigade level need to listen to the line noncommissioned officers in their subordinate units. Junior leaders in the field, officer and enlisted, are the only ones who know the moral health of their units—the squads and platoons that do the fighting, and in which the right and wrong actions take place. Senior commanders need to empower junior battlefield leaders to do what they feel is *ethically* necessary to complete the mission, and that means casting off warriors who may be courageous but are morally unsuited for the wars we now fight.

Our military was once seriously plagued by illegal drugs, racism, and sexism. Education and vigilance may still be required in these areas, but we've largely moved past these forms of wrong conduct inasmuch as they threaten the force and the mission. Much of the progress in these areas has been the result of proscribed and encouraged intolerance. We certainly can't screen for immorality using random urinalysis, and it may not be feasible to have an 800 number for improper shooting or mistreatment of local detainees, but you get the idea. Our regional and brigade commanders must find better ways for their field units to communicate wrong conduct up the chain of command. Senior commanders must also find a way to communicate the consequences of wrong conduct on the insurgent battlefield to warriors in the ground-combat units. Senior-level commanders must not only be aware of what's taking place in the squads and platoons, they must also empower their junior leaders to effectively deal with it.

Sam Walton got it right when he advocated management by walking around. To know what's going on in the retail business, you have to get out of your office and visit with the troops—the retail clerks. In *One Bullet Away*, Nate Fick, then a lieutenant, wrote of moving about his platoon's perimeter one night to check with those on sentry duty. He knew his platoon sergeant usually did this, but it was a chance for him to visit with his men individually and to see how they were getting along. On one of those nocturnal circuits, he slid into a foxhole with two marine lance corporals, only to find (then) Major General James Mattis there with them. Now that's walking around! The operation of a combat sector, let alone the running of a division or a brigade, is a complex business. There are protocols, not the least of which is to avoid micromanaging your subordinates. Nonetheless, all leaders have to find a way to get out and check the moral perimeters of their units.

Junior leaders, you have a continuous and never-ending duty to tend to the moral health of your men. Most of those in your units and those coming to your units are steeped in a tradition of brand consciousness. Brands and logos are drilled into young Americans by repetitive imprinting from the media and advertising. You must make honor and right conduct a part of your unit's branding; impress your men with the idea that wrong conduct tarnishes your brand and is a form of disloyalty to all warriors who fight for the brand. Train them, trust them, hold them to standard.

Last but not least, a word for all those PFCs and lance corporals—the trigger pullers, men who are among the best and bravest warriors America has ever put in the field. Please know that I and the warriors of my generation stand in your shadow. You guys are the greatest. I ask only that you keep your honor on par with your marvelous professional skill. If some pirate in your unit tries to minimize you or tarnish your honor, take a stand—take action. To each one of our nation's good and honorable warriors, God bless and good hunting.

Appendix I
General David H. Petraeus on Values

HEADQUARTERS
MULTI-NATIONAL FORCE - IRAQ
BAGHDAD, IRAQ
APO AE 09342-1400

10 May 2007

Soldiers, Sailors, Airmen, Marines, and Coast Guardsmen serving
in Multi-National Force-Iraq:

Our values and the laws governing warfare teach us to respect
human dignity, maintain our integrity, and do what is right. Adherence to our values distinguishes us from our enemy. This fight
depends on securing the population, which must understand that
we—not our enemies—occupy the moral high ground. This strategy has shown results in recent months. Al Qaeda's indiscriminate
attacks, for example, have finally started to turn a substantial proportion of the Iraqi population against it.

In view of this, I was concerned by the results of a recently released
survey conducted last fall in Iraq that revealed an apparent unwilling-
ness on the part of some US personnel to report illegal actions taken
by fellow members of their units. The study also indicated that a small
percentage of those surveyed may have mistreated noncombatants.
This survey should spur reflection on our conduct in combat.

I fully appreciate the emotions that one experiences in Iraq. I
also know firsthand the bonds between members of the "brother-

hood of the close fight." Seeing a fellow trooper killed by a barbaric enemy can spark frustration, anger, and a desire for immediate revenge. As hard as it might be, however, we must not let these emotions lead us—or our comrades in arms—to commit hasty, illegal actions. In the event that we witness or hear of such actions, we must not let our bonds prevent us from speaking up.

Some may argue that we would be more effective if we sanctioned torture or other expedient methods to obtain information from the enemy. They would be wrong. Beyond the basic fact that such actions are illegal, history shows that they also are frequently neither useful nor necessary. Certainly, extreme physical action can make someone "talk;" however, what the individual says may be of questionable value. In fact, our experience in applying the interrogation standards laid out in the Army Field Manual (2-22.3) on Human Intelligence Collector Operations that was published last year shows that the techniques in the manual work effectively and humanely in eliciting information from detainees.

We are, indeed, warriors. We train to kill our enemies. We are engaged in combat, we must pursue the enemy relentlessly, and we must be violent at times. What sets us apart from our enemies in this fight, however, is how we behave. In everything we do, we must observe the standards and values that dictate that we treat noncombatants and detainees with dignity and respect. While we are warriors, we are also all human beings. Stress caused by lengthy deployments and combat is not a sign of weakness; it is a sign that we are human. If you feel such stress, do not hesitate to talk to your chain of command, your chaplain, or a medical expert.

We should use the survey results to renew our commitment to the values and standards that make us who we are and to spur re-examination of these issues. Leaders, in particular, need to discuss these issues with their troopers—and, as always, they need to set the right example and strive to ensure proper conduct. We should never underestimate the importance of good leadership and the difference it can make.

Thanks for what you continue to do. It is an honor to serve with each of you.

DAVID H. PETRAEUS
GENERAL, UNITED STATES ARMY
COMMANDING

Appendix II

Statements of Service Core Values

United States Army

Loyalty, Duty, Respect, Selfless service, Honor, Integrity, and Personal courage.

United States Air Force

Integrity first, Service before self, and Excellence in all we do.

United States Navy and Marine Corps

Honor, Courage, Commitment.

United States Coast Guard

Honor, Respect, Devotion to duty.

United States Special Operations Command

Integrity, Courage, Competence, and Creativity.

Appendix III
Statements of Service/Service-Component Credos

The Soldier's Creed (U.S. Army)

I am an American Soldier.

I am a Warrior and a member of a team. I serve the people of the United States and live the Army Values.

I will always place the mission first.

I will never accept defeat.

I will never quit.

I will never leave a fallen comrade.

I am disciplined, physically and mentally tough, trained and proficient in my warrior tasks and drills. I always maintain my arms, my equipment and myself.

I am an expert and I am a professional.

I stand ready to deploy, engage, and destroy the enemies of the United States of America in close combat.

I am a guardian of freedom and the American way of life.

I am an American Soldier.

The Creed of the U.S. Marine (The Rifleman's Creed)

This is my rifle.
There are many like it but this one is mine.

My rifle is my best friend. It is my life.
I must master it as I master my life.

My rifle, without me, is useless. Without my rifle, I am
useless. I must fire my rifle true. I must shoot straighter
than my enemy who is trying to kill me. I must shoot
him before he shoots me. I will . . .

My rifle and myself know that what counts in this war
is not the rounds we fire, the noise of our burst, nor the
smoke we make. We know that it is the hits that count.
We will hit . . .

My rifle is human, even as I, because it is my life.
Thus, I will learn it as a brother. I will learn its weakness, its strength, its parts, its accessories, its sights and
its barrel. . . . I will keep my rifle clean and ready, even
as I am clean and ready. We will become part of each
other. We will . . .

Before God I swear this creed. My rifle and myself are
the defenders of my country. We are the masters of our
enemy. We are the saviors of my life.

So be it, until victory is America's and there is no
enemy, but peace.

The Sailor's Creed (U.S. Navy)

I am a United States Sailor.

I will support and defend the Constitution of the United States of America and I will obey the orders of those appointed over me.

I represent the fighting spirit of the Navy and those who have gone before me to defend freedom and democracy around the world.

I proudly serve my country's Navy combat team with Honor, Courage and Commitment.

I am committed to excellence and the fair treatment of all.

The Airman's Creed (U.S. Air Force)

I am an American Airman.
I am a Warrior.
I have answered my nation's call.

I am an American Airman.
My mission is to fly, fight, and win.
I am faithful to a proud heritage,
a tradition of honor,
and a legacy of valor.

I am an American Airman.
Guardian of freedom and justice,
My nation's sword and shield,
Its sentry and avenger.
I defend my country with my life.

I am an American Airman:
Wingman, Leader, Warrior.
I will never leave an Airman behind.
I will never falter,
and I will not fail.

The U.S. Ranger Creed

Recognizing that I volunteered as a Ranger, fully knowing the hazards of my chosen profession, I will always endeavor to uphold the prestige, honor, and high esprit de corps of the Rangers.

Acknowledging the fact that a Ranger is a more elite soldier who arrives at the cutting edge of battle by land, sea, or air, I accept the fact that as a Ranger my country expects me to move further, faster, and fight harder than any other soldier.

Never shall I fail my comrades. I will always keep myself mentally alert, physically strong, and morally straight and I will shoulder more than my share of the task whatever it may be, one hundred percent and then some.

Gallantly will I show the world that I am a specially selected and well trained soldier. My courtesy to superior officers, neatness of dress, and care of equipment shall set the example for others to follow.

Energetically will I meet the enemies of my country. I shall defeat them on the field of battle for I am better trained and will fight with all my might. Surrender is not a Ranger word. I will never leave a fallen comrade to fall into the hands of the enemy and under no circumstances will I ever embarrass my country.

Readily will I display the intestinal fortitude required to fight on to the Ranger objective and complete the mission, though I be the lone survivor.

U.S. Army Special Forces Creed

I am an American Special Forces soldier!

I will do all that my nation requires of me.
I am a volunteer, knowing well the hazards of
my profession.

I serve with the memory of those
who have gone before me.
I pledge to uphold the honor and integrity of their
legacy in all I am—in all I do.

I am a warrior.
I will teach and fight whenever and
wherever my nation requires.
I will strive always to excel in every art and artifice of war.

I know that I will be called upon to perform
tasks in isolation,
far from familiar faces and voices.
With the help and guidance of my faith,
I will conquer my fears and succeed.

I will keep my mind and body clean, alert, and strong.
I will maintain my arms and equipment in
an immaculate state befitting a Special Forces soldier,
for this is my debt to those who depend on me.

I will not fail those with whom I serve.
I will not bring shame upon myself or the
Special Forces.

I will never leave a fallen comrade.
I will never surrender though I am the last.
If I am taken, I pray that I have the strength
to defy my enemy.

I am a member of my Nation's Chosen Soldiery.
I serve quietly, not seeking recognition or accolades.
My goal is to succeed in my mission—
and live to succeed again.

De Oppresso Liber

The Navy SEAL Creed

In times of war and uncertainty there is a special breed of warrior ready to answer our Nation's call. A common man with uncommon desire to succeed. Forged by adversity, he stands alongside America's finest special operation forces to serve his country, the American people, and protect their way of life. I am that man.

My Trident is a symbol of honor and heritage. Bestowed upon me by the heroes that have gone before, it embodies the trust of those I am sworn to protect. By wearing the Trident I accept the responsibility of my chosen profession and way of life. It is a privilege that I must earn every day.

My loyalty to Country and Team is beyond reproach. I humbly serve as a guardian to my fellow Americans always ready to defend those who are unable to defend themselves. I do not advertise the nature of my work, nor seek recognition for my actions. I voluntarily accept the inherent hazards of my profession, placing the welfare and security of others before my own.

I serve with honor on and off the battlefield. The ability to control my emotions and my actions, regardless of circumstance, sets me apart from other men. Uncompromising integrity is my standard. My character and honor are steadfast. My word is my bond.

We expect to lead and be led. In the absence of orders I will take charge, lead my teammates and accomplish the mission. I lead by example in all situations.

I will never quit. I persevere and thrive on adversity. My Nation expects me to be physically harder and mentally stronger than my enemies. If knocked down, I will get back up, every time. I will draw on every remaining ounce of strength to protect my teammates and to accomplish our mission. I am never out of the fight.

We demand discipline. We expect innovation. The lives of my teammates and the success of our mission depend on me—my technical skill, tactical proficiency, and attention to detail. My training is never complete.

We train for war and fight to win. I stand ready to bring the full spectrum of combat power to bear in order to achieve my mission and the goals established by my country. The execution of my duties will be swift and violent when required yet guided by the very principles that I serve to defend.

Brave men have fought and died building the proud tradition and feared reputation that I am bound to uphold. In the worst of conditions, the legacy of my teammates steadies my resolve and silently guides my every deed. I will not fail.

The Warrior Creed

Wherever I go,
everyone is a little bit safer
because I am there.
Wherever I am,
anyone in need has a friend.
Whenever I return home,
everyone is happy I am there.

—*Robert L. Humphrey, Iwo Jima Marine*

Appendix IV

U.S. Army Counterinsurgency Manual: Ethics Section

7-21. Article VI of the U.S. Constitution and Army Values, Soldier's Creed, and Core Values of the U.S. Marines all require the obedience to the law of armed conflict. They hold Soldiers and Marines to the highest standards of moral and ethical conduct. Conflict brings to bear enormous moral challenges, as well as the burden of life and death decisions with profound ethical considerations. Combat, including COIN and other forms of irregular warfare, often obligates Soldiers and Marines to choose the riskier course of action to minimize harm to noncombatants. This risk-taking is an essential part of the Warrior Ethos. In conventional conflicts, balancing competing responsibilities of mission accomplishment at least friendly cost with protection of noncombatants is difficult enough. Complex COIN operations place even tougher ethical demands on Marines, Soldiers, and their leaders.

7-22. Even in conventional operations, Soldiers and Marines are not permitted to use force disproportionately or indiscriminately. Typically, more force reduces risk. But the American military values obligate Soldiers and Marines to accomplish their missions while taking measures to limit the destruction, particularly in terms of harm to noncombatants, caused by military operations. This restriction is based on the belief that it is wrong to harm innocents, regardless of their citizenship.

7-23.　Limiting the misery caused by war requires combatants to consider certain rules, principles, and consequences that restrain the amount of force they may apply. At the same time, combatants are not required to take so much risk that they fail their mission or forfeit their lives. As long as their use of force is proportional to the gain to be achieved and discriminate in distinguishing between combatants and noncombatants, Soldiers and Marines may take actions where they knowingly risk, but do not intend, harm to noncombatants.

7-24.　Ethically speaking, COIN environments can be much more complex than conventional ones. Insurgency is more than combat between armed groups; it is a political struggle with a high level of violence intended to destabilize and ultimately overthrow a government. COIN forces using excessive force to limit short-term risk alienate local residents. In doing this, they deprive themselves of the support or tolerance of the populace. This situation is what the insurgents want. It increases the threat they pose. Sometimes lethal responses are counterproductive. At other times, they are essential. The art of command includes knowing the difference and directing the appropriate action.

7-25.　A key part of any insurgent's strategy is to attack their domestic and international opposition's political will. One of the insurgents' most effective means to undermine and erode political will is to portray their opposition as untrustworthy or illegitimate. These attacks are especially effective when insurgents can portray the opposition as unethical by their own standards. To combat these efforts, Soldiers and Marines treat noncombatants and detainees humanely and in accordance with America's values and internationally recognized human rights standards. In COIN, preserving noncombatant lives and dignity is central to mission accomplishment. This imperative creates a complex ethical environment that requires combatants to treat prohibitions against harming noncombatants as absolute.

Further, it can sometimes require combatants to forego lethal solutions altogether. In practical terms, this consideration means that mission accomplishment sometimes obligates combatants to act more like police than warriors. That requirement imposes a very different calculus for the use of force.

Appendix V
CQD Integrity Commitment for Training

Author's note: The following is taken from the
CQD Manual/Inner Warrior overview.

Training Integrity Intent and Purpose

Instructors and students must be dedicated to the training purpose of operational success in combat, and honor and righteous actions in life. Both instructors and students must commit the greatest effort to achieve this goal.

Objectives

- Remain motivated and positive to assure the highest quality training occurs.
- Be certain the best tactics and techniques are taught to attain success.

Operator Tenets

As a warrior, integrity must be one of the greatest attributes. It is the duty of the operators to:

- Ensure that purpose, patriotism and honor are at the forefront of operational service.
- Evaluate your skill level and make sure proficient skills are reinforced by positive acknowledgment. Be critical of mistakes and be willing to do what it takes to remediate them.
- Support and assist fellow operators in developing skills for their survival as well as the survival of others.

- Activate skills appropriately and justifiably in accordance with the intent and actions of the threat.
- Appreciate all persons who support you and your mission. Recognize the incredible achievements of those who paved the way for your success, encouraging leadership that is entrusted with the operational and personal accomplishments and safety of the teams.

Instructor Tenets

Instructors must place the operator first to secure welfare and dominance on the battlefield. Students rely on you to prepare for the fight. It is essential for instructors to:

- Teach at the appropriate level for students to comprehend and validate skills because that is what they must rely on in combat.
- Teach to a depth of understanding that is undeniable to the student as to what is most effective.
- Train the students as if they are family or loved ones and their lives depend on your commitment to their readiness.
- Remember you are accountable for the level of instruction presented.
- Assist fellow instructors in maintaining the quality of skills. Continuity and consistency are paramount.
- Demonstrate integrity and honor in the classroom as well as in life.
- Always have time for students' questions or after-class discussion/validation to verify tactics are clear.
- Keep an open mind so the students can be confident in the methods taught.
- Validate that students recognize the importance of a skill or theory, and have the ability to utilize it under stress.
- Always be professional and polite in relations with others. Every action will reflect on the Cadre.
- Know that at the conclusion of each course, as an instructor, you should have a clear conscience that you did your very

best for the student and the operational capability provided for our country.

- Train to the best of your ability and ensure the students understand the tactics and techniques taught.
- Be patient and do your best to clarify your point of view. The students may be accustomed to a myriad of techniques and theories that do not integrate operationally.
- Understand the tactics taught are providing the options the operators must rely upon, but in the actual fight it is always their call as to what skills to employ.

Student Tenets
The students' contribution to ensure course quality is as follows:

- Confirm that throughout training, all instruction is understood and proven.
- Always ask questions when unclear.
- Have an open mind while learning.
- Be responsible to personally deliver quality performance and support their teammates' efforts.
- Ensure the highest standards by communicating integrity infractions. The dedication of the students determines the performance level that can be achieved.

Integrity Training Process
Both instructors and students put forth the greatest effort to succeed and utilize the Clarification Options, when necessary, to achieve a successful understanding of the training.

Training Clarification Options
- Questions in and after class and on breaks
- Special sessions
- Validation exercises
- Integrity infractions
  — Undermining or negatively influencing training without utilizing clarification opportunities.

— Making false comments and statements about the training or others.
— Disparaging fellow operators.
— Manipulating discussion points that are not said in context to minimize others.

Infractions in integrity are grounds for dismissal. The integrity components are on a graded scale for overall operator performance.

Index

About the Author

DICK COUCH, a graduate of the U.S. Naval Academy, served on active duty with the Navy Underwater Demolition and SEAL teams for five years. While a platoon leader with SEAL Team One, he led one of the only POW rescues of the Vietnam War. In 1972 he joined the CIA and retired from the Naval Reserve in 1997 with the rank of captain. He has frequently appeared as a military expert on nationally syndicated TV and radio programs. In addition to many bestselling novels, he is the author of several works of nonfiction about the Navy SEALs and the Green Berets, including *Chosen Soldier, The Sheriff of Ramadi,* and *The Warrior Elite.* Captain Couch currently serves as a consultant on ethics to the Commander, U.S. Special Operations Command.

THE NAVAL INSTITUTE PRESS is the book-publishing arm of the U.S. Naval Institute, a private, nonprofit, membership society for sea service professionals and others who share an interest in naval and maritime affairs. Established in 1873 at the U.S. Naval Academy in Annapolis, Maryland, where its offices remain today, the Naval Institute has members worldwide.

Members of the Naval Institute support the education programs of the society and receive the influential monthly magazine *Proceedings* or the colorful bimonthly magazine *Naval History* and discounts on fine nautical prints and on ship and aircraft photos. They also have access to the transcripts of the Institute's Oral History Program and get discounted admission to any of the Institute-sponsored seminars offered around the country.

The Naval Institute's book-publishing program, begun in 1898 with basic guides to naval practices, has broadened its scope to include books of more general interest. Now the Naval Institute Press publishes about seventy titles each year, ranging from how-to books on boating and navigation to battle histories, biographies, ship and aircraft guides, and novels. Institute members receive significant discounts on the Press's more than eight hundred books in print.

Full-time students are eligible for special half-price membership rates. Life memberships are also available.

For a free catalog describing Naval Institute Press books currently available, and for further information about joining the U.S. Naval Institute, please write to:

Member Services
U.S. Naval Institute
291 Wood Road
Annapolis, MD 21402-5034
Telephone: (800) 233-8764
Fax: (410) 571-1703
Web address: www.usni.org